PETS
& their
PEOPLE

PETS
& their
PEOPLE

Charles Foster

BODLEIAN
LIBRARY
PUBLISHING

For Jimmy and Melanie Watt, and of course Jonnie

First published in 2025 by Bodleian Library Publishing
Broad Street, Oxford OX1 3BG
www.bodleianshop.co.uk

ISBN 978 1 85124 646 5

PUBLISHER Samuel Fanous
MANAGING EDITOR Susie Foster
EDITOR Janet Phillips
PICTURE EDITOR Leanda Shrimpton
COVER DESIGN by Dot Little at the Bodleian Library
DESIGNED & TYPESET by Lucy Morton of illuminati in 11½ on 16 Garamond
PRINTED & BOUND by Livonia Print, Latvia, on 115 gsm Munken Premium Cream paper

British Library Catalogue in Publishing Data
A CIP record of this publication is available from the British Library

Contents

Acknowledgements

I am hugely grateful to many people, over many years, who have helped to formulate and/or mock my ideas. There are far too many to thank by name, but I need to mention specifically Amin Benaissa, Lanisha Butterfield, Andrew Dunning, Janet Foot, Niko Kontovas, Hugo Lacoue-Labarthe, Colin McIlroy, Emma Mathieson, Emma O'Bryen, Dan O'Neill, Keith and Emily Powell, Claire and Mike Smith, Kian Swingler, Barney Taylor, Peter Toth, Alasdair Watson, Mark and Sue West, Amy Ellis Winter, the Fellows of Exeter College, Oxford, and an anonymous reviewer. Discussions with Greger Larson radically reshaped my understanding of domestication in general and cat domestication in particular.

Emma Searle provided the splendid translations of Catullus on pp. 67 and 114, and of the Roman grave stele (p. 120 and PLATE 2).

At Bodleian Library Publishing, particular thanks to Samuel Fanous, who helped greatly in finalizing the architecture of the book; my wonderful editor, Janet Phillips; and my picture editor, Leanda Shrimpton. Chris Fletcher and Maddy Slaven at the Bodleian Library have been relentlessly patient and inspirational, and Lucy Morton at illuminati guided the book smoothly through the production process.

Preface

Animals and humans are two of the most mysterious things in the cosmos. The notion of relationship is even more mysterious. So to write a book about the relationship between animals and humans is hubristic madness. I can make only two points in my defence. The first is that I was asked to do it, and the second is that I can't think of many subjects that matter more.

I suspect that most writers, academic and otherwise, only ever write about one thing. That's certainly true of me. Everything I've written has been an attempt to find out what sort of creatures humans are. The issue matters for many reasons – not the least of which is that I am a human, and can't know what it means to live and behave well if I have no idea what I am. This book is part of that project. Pet dogs, cats, guinea pigs, hamsters and snakes can give a far more shrewd and articulate answer to the question 'What is a human?' than most human literature – constipated as that literature is with presumption, vanity, fear and exhaustion.

I doubt that we can see anything worth seeing (or anything at all) by looking at it directly. The edge of our consciousness and the far frontier of our understanding are the only useful vantage points, and the very corners of our eyes the only useful sensory receptors. It is from those places, with those receptors, that I've tried to see the very weird business of pet ownership – of, that is, the 'ownership' of animals by humans, and of humans by animals. There are, therefore, despatches from prehistory and the future; from dogs who watch the birth of saints, and from ghost cats; from humans rolling merrily with their dogs in a summer field and from those who hang their hamster's ashes next to their heart. Mediaeval illuminated manuscripts jostle internet pet memorial sites.

Since nobody stands much chance of saying anything worthwhile about a relationship apart from the parties to it, I've tried to let owners speak for themselves – even when that leaves me open to the allegation of mawkishness or voyeurism.

A word about etymology and definitions. The origins of the word 'pet' are obscure. Katherine Grier notes that it may derive from the French *petit* (small), and that it was first applied to humans but by the early sixteenth century denoted a spoiled, indulged, favoured child.[1] By the middle of that century it included, according to the *Oxford English Dictionary*, animals 'domesticated or tamed and kept for pleasure or companionship', and by the early seventeenth century had become a verb – though it did not denote human sexual activity until the early twentieth century.

In this book I deal mainly with non-agricultural and domesticated rather than tamed animals. Domestication and taming are not the same. Elephants can be tamed; they cannot be domesticated.

Phajaan is a Thai expression describing one method of elephant-taming, used in Thailand and Myanmar. It can be translated as 'elephant crushing', and involves the close confinement of captured baby elephants – confinement so close that they cannot move at all. It is often combined with beatings. The aim is to crush the elephant's spirit. The result will be a tame, but not domesticated, elephant. Domestication, as I use the idea, denotes a coalition between human and animal for which the animal is temperamentally suited. A dog's spirit does not need to be crushed before the dog enters into a coalition with its owner.

I suppose there are two ways of writing a book about an infinitely huge and complex subject. The first is to write a book that is infinitely long. The second is to write a book that is very short – on the basis that the less of it there is, the less it will misrepresent the subject and hopefully, too, that the hubris of writing anything at all might be seen by the vengeful gods as less culpable.

I have written a short book.

The harder and the longer I have looked at the phenomenon of pet ownership, the more mysterious it has become. I'm reassured rather than disillusioned by that. That's surely how it (and, for that matter, everything) should be if we're looking properly.

ONE

The weirdness of pets, and how to explore it

We kill rats, mice, flies and cockroaches whenever we can, but invite huge numbers of other animals into our homes.

The costs of the invitation are staggering.

Pet ownership is so common that we do not see its weirdness.

In the UK there are 13.5 million pet dogs, 12.5 million cats, 1.5 million indoor birds, 1 million rabbits, 700,000 tortoises and turtles, 700,000 pet horses, 700,000 guinea pigs, 600,000 hamsters, and 600,00 snakes. Some 36 per cent of households have a dog, 29 per cent have a cat, 21 per cent have indoor fish tanks, and 13 per cent have outdoor fish ponds.[1]

Something significant is going on. It needs to be explained.

Here is another indication of that significance.

Honey's is a UK-based pet food company. Its values and ethos are impeccable. But, just as with human food, values and ethos come at a price.

Honey's can make dog food to order. 'Honey's bespoke' is 'like having your own private canine chef'. Here are their estimates of the monthly costs for bespoke food for various sizes of dog, boxed into meal portions, assuming that two portions are fed per day, and including next-day delivery by DHL. Each is assumed to have no health problems. The figures seem very reasonable for the quality, quantity and effort.[2]

	30 KG 7-YEAR-OLD DOG	17 KG 7-YEAR-OLD MALE DOG	5 KG 7-YEAR-OLD MALE DOG
ORGANIC/ WILD: COOKED	£866.99	£528.93	£314.75
ORGANIC/ WILD: RAW	£762.82	£327.89	£255.05
FREE-RANGE/ PASTURE-FED: COOKED	£689.96	£440.42	£277.88
FREE-RANGE/ PASTURE-FED	£586.73	£278.20	£224.36

For perspective: in June 2023 the average spend on food in the UK was £44.70 per person per week. That's £193.60 a month.[3]

Pasture-fed, organic, wild: we want for our pets what we want for ourselves.

Why do we do it? How can we possibly think it's worth it? What does it tell us about ourselves?

Many pet owners talk about companionship, about having someone around who is faithful: who won't let them down, unlike capricious and treacherous humans. Almost all pet owners talk to their pets, and assume the pet understands. Many think the pet talks back. Other owners, more breezily, say that the dog gets them out of the house and keeps them fit. Others talk about health too, and about the sense of calm they feel when they stroke the dog.

I don't doubt the genuineness of these answers. But they don't go to the heart of the issue. Far from it. They magnify the strangeness of pet ownership. Why should those sorts of benefit result from a relationship with species very different from our own?

To be sure, there are plenty of examples of important relationships between different species. Fungi and plants exist in a sophisticated confederation which ensures that each has the necessary nutrients. Small fish on coral reefs pick parasites from the scales of larger fish. We ourselves are vast, fulminating ecosystems – heaving with bacteria and viruses and fungi upon which we depend, and which depend on us. But there's nothing in the natural world quite like pet ownership. I doubt a shark sees a remora as a pet. A chimpanzee in the forests of DRC might play for a while with a captured bird, but soon it will get bored and bite off its head and eat it. We don't usually eat our pets.

Pets can be deadly: think of all those headlines describing how a bulldog (designed to hang on to the nose of a tortured bull) has mauled a toddler. We think of ourselves as bird-lovers, but fund cats, who kill more than 25 million garden birds a year in the UK alone.[4] Dogs deposit tonnes of faeces onto British pavements every year: every responsible dog-owner, in looking forward to the daily walk, looks forward also to a plastic bag full of steaming dung.

Tapeworms in dog faeces can cause blindness. Toxoplasma, carried by cats, can cause miscarriage, flu-like illness and blindness. Rabies kills around 60,000 humans each year: dogs account for around 99 per cent of human rabies cases.[5] While cats rub themselves on your legs, dogs mate with your legs – or more usually with the legs of the fastidious visitor you're trying to impress. Dogs sometimes really do eat the homework. Cats sharpen their claws on priceless furniture and the smell of their urine defies tectonic industrial cleaners. When a cat bites you it injects bacteria deep into the neat hole it creates, and when the hole closes over you'll have an abscess.

The dog, when it's finished with the visitor's leg, will look into her face with post-coital satisfaction and give her a blast of bad breath despite the anti-halitotic diet the vet prescribed, and despite the scale and polish it had, at eye-watering expense, just last week. The cat hair makes it impossible for any asthmatic to sleep on the sofa.

The expense of kennels, and the separation anxiety from which the dog suffers, mean that holidays aren't viable, though the neighbours (with whom you've fallen out because of the barking) are desperate for you to go. Every morning when you go to work the dog looks at you with those big liquid eyes, and you feel guilty all day for having abandoned it.

If you have smaller creatures – the hamsters, guinea pigs, tortoises, budgies, rabbits or mice the children begged for, promised to look after, hugged or admired for half an hour and then forgot – you'll wonder why. It'll be you who cleans out the cages and you who does the consoling when the animal dies (they die a lot, these kinds of animal) and the children are suddenly devoted after all, and devastated. You'll dig the hole and pretend to believe in animal souls as your daughter puts the shoebox into the earth, intones a liturgy and marks the plot with a cross, making it impossible to use that part of the garden for the onions you'd planned to put there.

The cat, having finished off the wild birds, will eat the hamster.

If you have more exotic pets – snakes, perhaps, or tarantulas – they'll escape. You know they will. And it will create a major incident, involving sleepless nights, bad dreams, and very possibly the police. It's very strange indeed.

I've wondered for a long time what this strangeness says about us: about me, and whether or not I should live petlessly. This book is an attempt to explore the strangeness: to get beyond the usual reasons given for pet ownership. It will involve looking at those reasons, and the ways those reasons were articulated across regions, ages and cultures. But that's not enough.

Not only is the answer to the question 'why pets?' not at all obvious; it's not at all obvious where we should look. How, then, should we ensure that we've looked in all the conceivable places?

The obvious way, it seemed to me, was to look at the role of pets in all the chronological stages of human life, from birth to death and beyond. So that's what I've done here, and that's how the book is structured. I'd hoped that the answer might be clear from an examination of pets in childhood – perhaps illuminated by a bit of Freud. If so, I thought, very good: it could be a very short book – little more than an essay – quickly written and quickly read. But it didn't turn out that way at all – though this is indeed a short book. It wasn't that childhood didn't contribute to an answer: it did. But it showed that the answer was far weirder and more complex than I'd imagined, and pointed me on to the next stage of human life for further comment. And the same thing happened there. And so on, until I'd gone beyond the grave.

Only then, when all the evidence was in, and I was looking back at a whole human life and the place of animals in it, did I start to see the faint outline of an answer starting to form. I sketch in the final chapter what I saw.

Whoever would have thought that dogs, cats and budgies could signify so much? I certainly didn't.

TWO

How the animals got into our homes

God, at least in the Judaeo-Christian tradition, is ambivalent about pet ownership.

He is not at all ambivalent about animals. He created them, says the book of Genesis, and declared in the first of the two creation stories not only that they were good, but that the whole cosmic ecosystem of which they were a part was *very* good.[1]

In the second of the two stories Adam, the first man, names the animals. God had given Adam general sovereignty over the created order, but now Adam looked into the eyes of each animal and decided what he, Adam, thought that animal should be. A new, special, customized relationship was formed – one which makes our animal abuses all the more shameful and our functional relationships with animals all the more fecund. Surely the animals acknowledged their names, as modern dogs do, and surely there was the electric reciprocity known to all dog owners and thought to exist by all cat owners.[2]

It was not good for man to be alone, thought God. It seems that the original plan was for the animals to be man's companions. But, even with that reciprocity, the animals were not enough for Adam. For him 'no suitable helper' was found amongst the furry and feathered and scaly creatures around him, and so the second human, Eve, was fashioned from Adam's rib.[3] Animals, says the story, are no substitute for human company. Animals give something different from humans – different in kind and degree.

The animals' names were the first words uttered by a human. But the first recorded conversation was with an animal too. It did not go well. It was, of course, the calamitous discourse between Eve and the serpent, which led to the expulsion of Adam and Eve from the garden, a painful dislocation of the harmonious, ecologically balanced, lotus-eating relationships that the humans had had with the non-humans, and the birth of arduous agriculture: 'By the sweat of your brow shall you eat bread', declared God.[4] There had been no need for sweat before.

The Judaeo-Christian tradition has been generally suspicious since of humans talking to animals. It has happened on unusual occasions, such as the fraught exchange between Balaam and his ass,[5] and a few spiritual superstars, such as Solomon[6] and St Francis, knew the language of non-humans. But not only has talking to animals not been encouraged for the rank and file; for much of Christian history, as we will see, talking to animals was likely to put you on top of a bonfire or at the bottom of the village pond.

'Dog', in the Bible, is usually an insult. Dogs come out well in only one quasi-biblical story – in the book of Tobit, where a faithful dog has a trot-on part, accompanying the protagonist Tobias as he looks for a cure for his father's blindness. The book of Tobit didn't make the cut for the canonical Bible.

Dog ownership has traditionally been unusual in Orthodox Jewish homes (though cats were commonly kept as mousers). There is no actual prohibition on dogs as such – though dangerous or even frightening dogs are proscribed.[7] Leviticus declares that it is wrong to damage an animal's reproductive organs,[8] which outlaws castration and spaying, so making dog ownership less manageable. The Chabad Lubavitch movement suggests that one reason for the relative unpopularity of pets in Orthodox households may be that 'pets are generally non-kosher animals, and there is a preference for seeing kosher images to whatever degree possible.'[9]

There are texts in Islamic Hadith indicating that dogs should not be kept except for guarding or hunting. The ninth-century collectors of Hadith, Muhammad Al-Bukhari and Muslim ibn al-Hajjaj, record that the Prophet said: 'The angels do not enter a house in which there is a dog.'[10] This may be a rule more observed in the Gulf states than elsewhere. Elsewhere in the Islamic world there is often a taboo attached to dog saliva rather than the dog itself. A hand licked by a dog may be regarded as ritually unclean in a way that a hand licked by a cat is not.[11] Pet ownership is otherwise permitted in Islam – with stern injunctions about the obligation to treat animals kindly. Al-Bukhari and Muslim say that the Prophet himself played with a pet nightingale,[12] and the fourteenth–fifteenth-century scholar Al-Hafiz Ibn Hajar interpreted this story as indicating that 'it is permissible for children to play with birds, and it is permissible to spend money on permissible things that will entertain children, and it is permissible to keep birds in cages and the like, and to clip the wings of birds'.[13]

The world of the early chapters of Genesis is the Neolithic. It knew all about dogs. They had already been around for a long time. Just how long is debated furiously, with lots of footnotes. The minutiae of the debate need not concern us. What matters more is how they came to be by our firesides. Enough is clear for our purposes about both the when and the how.

★

Dogs are modified wolves. *Very* modified wolves. Wolves, for instance, have tiny *levator anguli oculi* muscles around their eyes. In dogs, these muscles are huge, which means that dogs, unlike wolves, can make their eyes seem bigger and more expressive, exposing the white sclera and flashing love, alarm and apparent sympathy at us. Jonathan Balcombe suggests that we treat fish with such callousness compared to mammals and birds because fish have no eyelids, and therefore can't signal their distress to us.[14] It is plausible.

We might be misreading many of our dogs' cues (their world, after all, is primarily an olfactory world: a third of a dog's brain mass is devoted to smell, compared to 5 per cent of ours), but as long as we feel we understand them – that we share a common language – we will bond with them as we would not with (perhaps) equally emotional wolves which just happen to have relatively immobile eyelids.

We have, in fact, learned some genuine Dr Dolittle or Solomonic skills. We don't quite speak dog language, but just as we talk to babies in infant-directed speech – more slowly than usual, and with a high-pitched voice and greater pitch variation – so we talk to our dogs in a similar, babyish-doggy way (it's called pet-directed speech) and we now know that adult dogs respond better to it than to normal speech.[15] Evolution seems to have favoured our ability to speak to dogs because it is to our advantage to be bound intimately to them. It's to a dog's advantage, too, to know human words and concepts, and they do. An average modern dog can learn 165 words (the top 20 per cent can learn 250), count up to 4 or 5, and detect errors in simple calculations – such as 1 + 1 = 1.[16]

We might be misreading our dogs, but they are closer to us than any other animals. So close, in fact, that it is often hard to know where the dog ends and the owner begins: they seem to be one indivisible unit. Dogs expect to cooperate with their owners in the performance of tasks. Puppies, indeed, appear to prefer humans to dogs, and to believe humans rather than the evidence of their own senses. Even if their eyes tell them that a ball is under a particular cup, a human's insistence that the ball is under another cup will trump the dog's own eyes. Dogs follow human pointing. Faced with a problem, they may look at their human for help.

Dogs are better behaved when they play with humans than when they play with other dogs: they show far more give and take, and are less aggressive. And, as we'll see, humans certainly feel happier when they are with their dogs than when they're not. We needn't rely on anecdote for that conclusion: concentrations of the bonding hormone, oxytocin, which produces a feeling of well-being, rise 130 per cent in dogs and 300 per cent in owners when they stare into one another's eyes for half an hour.[17] Other compounds are in play too – notably our natural opiates, endorphins. Endorphin production is powerfully stimulated by the grooming of our hairy areas, and may be stimulated too by the feel of fur against our own skin. (It's interesting that we are less attracted to bald animals.) When you stroke your dog and are nuzzled by it, you may both be getting a heroin-like high. Opiates are powerfully addictive. You may be physically addicted to your dog, and go truly cold turkey when you are parted.

It's a curious alliance. Its roots go deep into our hunter–gatherer past.

★

One of the most eloquent finds from the Upper Palaeolithic is from the Chauvet cave, in the Ardèche, France. It is 26,000 years old and 230 feet long – a trail of two sets of footprints; a boy and a dog. The boy was perhaps 8 or 10 years old, and around 4½ feet tall. He was walking very close to the dog. His hand may have been on the dog's back. It would not be surprising, for the cave was dark and frightening then, as it is now, and dog-friends no doubt comforted then as they do now. The cave was lit, at best, with a torch dipped in bear fat, throwing predatory shadows onto the wall, but the child's steps were confident because the dog was there.[18]

When did dogs and humans first become friends? The estimates vary wildly – sometimes because scholars conflate domestication with taming or with mere proximity. It may have been have been more than 40,000 years ago, and there may have been two or more independent episodes of domestication. There are profound genetic differences between West Asian and East Asian dogs, which may reflect different origins.

How did it happen? Again, we don't know, but no doubt the fostering of wolf cubs orphaned by human hunters played some part. Dingo pups are often adopted, and women are known to breastfeed puppies in many parts of the world, including the Andaman Islands, the Brazilian and Venezuelan Amazon, Australia and Arctic Canada. Another possible driver of domestication, though, is far more disgusting.

Dogs like eating human faeces – so much so that our dung may have been the main draw pulling dogs into our orbit. Some 20 per cent of the diet of modern Ethiopian village dogs was found to be human faeces.[19] Our faeces are good nourishment: 'comparable to the upper range of energy content for mammal tissue, vegetables and fruit'. The link with wolves may have been forged by our inefficient, wasteful guts, which lose many useful calories, and by our generally wasteful habits, disgorging unused bones and other food onto the midden. Wolves have very catholic digestive tracts which cope happily with fruit, vegetables and cereals as well as caribou and moose flesh. The faecal fast food of a human camp, some say, must have been irresistible. Other scholars differ, contending that Pleistocene communities were too small to be a significant food source for wolves.

However the attachment occurred, once the wolves had attached themselves to the human community, the traits that allowed them to come even closer – to get the advantages of even more succulent waste and a berth by the campfire – would have been selected for very efficiently. Those traits would have included docility, the ability to work out what humans wanted, a desire to please, and the other complex skills associated with cooperation. These characteristics can emerge amazingly fast, as the Russian scientist Dmitry Belyaev, who bred silver foxes, selecting specifically for tameness, demonstrated in the 1950s. In a mere four generations there was a visible change in behaviour, and within forty generations (about twenty-five years) the foxes showed all the behavioural characteristics of domestic dogs. They were less excitable than they had been; levels of the stress hormone, cortisol, were half what they had been; and these new foxes looked and smelt like dogs. They had curly tails, floppy ears and short noses, and they turned white – the colour of surrender.

They didn't surrender only their colour. If you abandon the wild, entering into a cosy contract that involves less walking, foraging and killing, and more lounging, there is a steep price to pay. Domestication infantilizes and dumbs down. Domestic animals of all species tend to keep juvenile characteristics into adulthood. Accounting for body size, dog brains are three-quarters the size of wolf brains. It happened to us too. Our brains are 10 per cent smaller than they were 10,000 years ago. Since dogs have played a big part in our own domestication, some of the blame for our shrunken brains lies with them.[20]

*

Dogs have domesticated us at least as much as we have domesticated them. Most of us are thoroughly and disgracefully domesticated, but most of today's dogs are not. There are thought to be between 700 million and a billion dogs in the world. Most are unowned, feral creatures, scavenging on the edges of human settlements, but truncated cognitively by association with us; by having traded their wild heritage for the pottage of ease.

Over the course of human history a far higher proportion of humans have had dogs than dogs have had intimate humans. And 'our' dogs have made us what we are. Natural selection favoured humans who got on with dogs. John Bradshaw writes:

> Those of our ancestors who understood animals would have prospered at the expense of those who could not. Thirty thousand years ago they would have been better hunters; 20,000 years ago they would have harnessed dogs' abilities to guard their homesteads and improve their detection of quarry; 8,000 years ago, their food stores, protected by cats, would have lasted, while those of their neighbours disappeared into the mouths of mice. People with the capacity to form relationships with individual animals would, probably more by accident than design, have protected them from mating with their wild counterparts, thereby preventing dilution of the genetic material that distinguished useful domestic stock with the genes of wild ancestors and thus preserving the blood lines that persist right through to the present day. Those who carried the genes for a facility with animals may also have found favour because this skill acted as a proxy for probable good parenting.[21]

Dogs brought down gazelles and hares, snarled at the predatory eyes at the edge of the firelight, herded our domestic ruminants and pigs, ate rubbish and the rats that harboured disease, dragged us on sledges into areas we would never otherwise have known and kept us warm at night as the snow fell, guarded the settlements when the hunters were away (allowing for the separation of the sexes), tracked outlaws (so cementing the rule of law), were used as weapons, political icons and advertising gimmicks, supplanted our children in our affections, and allowed us to continue to believe that we were really wild (since we had wolves in our centrally heated bungalows). Dogs are high achievers.

Nothing about humans is *only* material. We can't be described adequately just in terms of equations governing energy expenditure or gene flow. We are metaphysical as well as physical animals. A central reality of the dog–human journey, writes Laura Hobgood-Oster, is that it has at its core

> a religious connection. Which also means that the canine–human story has the questions of who humans think they are in the world, and of what truly matters to them. Denying the role of dogs not only diminishes dogs, but diminishes humanity. Humans are essentially connected to other species; they cannot live without intimate companionship with others. It makes humans human.[22]

Has the dog–human coalition been good for humans and dogs? Well, arguably. But not for many other species (though one might make a case for sheep, goats and cattle, whose domestication was doubtless helped by the dogs that herded them). Together, dogs and humans have hunted many species to and over the edge of extinction. Together we may have devastated – by about 11,000 years ago – the late Pleistocene megafauna of north America. (Some lay the blame mainly at the door of climate change.) If it hadn't been for dogs, mastodons might be swaying today up Fifth Avenue, and giant beavers building dams in Central Park. We invited wild wolves into our lives, and together we conspired to kill or sublimate wildness in ourselves, in the newly tamed wolves and in the world outside. The conspiracy didn't *quite* come off, but it has done a lot of damage.

The human–dog relationship has changed over time. It began as a partnership for controlling the wild, and a by-product of that partnership was our own un-wilding. Now it is a partnership for keeping us in touch with our residual wildness: for suppressing the tameness we despise in ourselves. This great conversation between the wild and the tame *is* human history, human psychology, human politics and human sociology. And it is also, and not at all coincidentally, dog history, psychology, politics and sociology.

Humans are extremely successful survival machines (only very recently have we displayed suicidal blindness about how to endure as a species), but we have never been *merely* machines. We are splendid tool-makers, and soon grow to love our tools.

In 1914, workers in a quarry in the Oberkassel suburb of Bonn discovered a Magdalenian grave (from around 14,000 years ago) containing grave goods and the bones of a 50-year-old man, a young woman of perhaps 20–25 years, and a 27–28-week-old dog. The dog's teeth showed that between 19 and 27 weeks of age it had had three debilitating bouts of canine distemper. It would have been very ill during that time, no good for hunting or guarding, and would have needed careful nursing to survive. It was loved for itself – not for its utility.

Loved too, it seems, was the four- or five-month-old puppy under the hand of a Natufian skeleton in the Jordan Valley – a puppy that has been patted for the last 12,000 years – and the small, arthritic, bad-toothed old dog buried at the feet of a young Roman-era woman in Carthage. The Carthaginian dog must have had foul breath, and would have had to be carried round and fed soft food. Any coldly calculating utilitarian would have killed it: the Carthaginian woman kept it going for years.

The utilitarian would also have protested against changes in dog size and shape. The wolf size and shape are ideally suited to *useful* dogs, yet by the Mediterranean Bronze Age (say 4,000 years ago), domestic wolves had morphed into dachshund-like creatures, from whose loins quickly sprang a dazzling variety of small, picturesque, apparently loveable house dogs who must have yapped impotently at the jackals and never got anywhere near a deer.

Useful dogs survived and thrived too. Pharaonic Egypt, for instance, bred stately gazehounds, and hunters have always prized dogs' wonderful noses.

There is no clear line between useful dogs and pets. Pleistocene hunters no doubt used their hunting dogs as pillows and fed them pieces of liver they would have liked to eat themselves. Nineteenth-century English squires drank claret by the fire, surrounded by their pointers and retrievers. We explore this eloquent phenomenon in Chapter 5, but the main focus of this book is on pets whose sole purpose is… well, what is it?

*

Modern cats pose that question very acutely.

Their story differs from that of dogs, because of their different physiology and psychology. They are committed carnivores, as dogs are not. They do not salivate at the smell of human dung or rejoice when a pot of rice is scraped out onto the ground. Only a small part of our waste is interesting to them. And, unlike wolves and dogs, they are not hard-wired for co-operation. They are solitary, slinking hunters, without the neurological software for divining our intentions, or any enthusiasm for joining us in a shared project. Even if they wanted to be grafted into us as dogs are, the graft would not take.

Today's domestic cats are descendants of the African wildcat, *Felis sylvestris lybica,* a sandy grey animal that kills birds, small mammals, reptiles and rodents throughout Africa and as far east as Xinjiang and Rajasthan. Domestic cats were long thought to be creatures of the Neolithic; of the mouse-infested grain silos of the Fertile Crescent, and to have spread from there to the rest of the world because of their value as rodent-killers on ships.[23] Their first known port of call outside the mainland Near East, says the conventional account, was Cyprus, to which they must have gone by sea. On Cyprus, just 40 cm from a human (of unknown sex) buried 9,500 years ago, an eight-month-old cat was buried too, its body oriented westwards like the human. The cat (says the story) surely wasn't buried just to keep down vermin in the land beyond the sunset: it was giving the human the stand-offish, one-sided companionship which is the way of cats down the ages.

It is a great story. Unfortunately it is almost certainly wrong. Recent evidence has cast serious doubt on the identification of the cat as a domestic cat. If domestic cats were on Cyprus in 7500 BC, it is inconceivable that they would not have reached mainland Europe shortly afterwards. But they don't. They don't get there for thousands of years. The exact time of their arrival is unclear.

The real story probably starts in Egypt.[24] There is evidence from pre-Dynastic Hierokonopolis, around 5,700 years ago, of human control over cat reproduction. Six juvenile cats were found in a single burial, with age profiles indicating human intervention. This is 2,000 years before we commonly see cat remains and depictions in an unambiguously domestic context. But why were cats being pulled into the human fold? The answer, it seems, is not rodent-killing, but religion.

The goddess Bastet was worshipped in Egypt from at least 2800 BC until the Romans arrived (PLATE 1), and she had her own gigantic red granite city, Bubastis, in the Eastern Delta. When she was first depicted, in the third millennium BC, she had a lion's head. But her head changed. By the ninth to seventh centuries she had the head of an African wildcat.

Gods and goddesses demanded sacrifice. Think of worshippers in a Christian church, buying candles to place before an altar, an icon or a statue. Bastet worshippers did that with dead cats. Mummified cats became big business. Millions of them were produced – an enterprise that must have required vast cat farms. They were strangled or had their necks snapped before being crudely preserved and swathed in bandages.[25] This meant not (at first) that cats were pets, but that cats were popular and protected (except when Bastet demanded them).

The Bastet cult no doubt promoted both cat ownership (perhaps it was thought that Bastet would bless a cat-owing home) and ownership *by* cats, which is what always happens. Many Bastet temples were in arable areas, and cats no doubt quickly proved their worth as rodent-controllers. From there they wormed their way into the affections of at least some of us. Herodotus, writing in the mid fifth century BC, tells us that Egyptians would run into blazing buildings to save their cats (doubtless motivated both by religious devotion and genuine affection), and that when a cat died, all the human inhabitants of its house shaved their eyebrows as a mourning gesture. Dead cats were taken to Bubastis, embalmed, and buried in sacred receptacles.[26] There are many examples, too, over long periods of time, of Egyptians being interred with their cats. It is impossible and artificial to disentangle theology and love.

The Greeks conquered Egypt, and were themselves conquered by cats (a recurring motif in feline history), which were assimilated into the mythology and rites of Artemis, who was said to be able to take the form of a cat, and was closely associated with the moon. The same happened to the conquering Romans – for Artemis was conflated with the Roman goddess, Diana. Religion, then, continued to be the cats' main vehicle in their spread north.[27] We see them, for instance, as the companions of the Norse goddess, Freyja. The sagas speak of wise women clothed in white cat fur, and cat bones appear in graves and cult sites throughout the Norse world.

Cats continued to be associated with basically *good* religion until the European Middle Ages. Then, as 'wise women' were demonized and denounced as witches, their cats were demonized too. In the Upper Palaeolithic a shaman's ability to transform into an animal had been celebrated. In mediaeval and early modern Europe a woman's ability (it was usually a woman) to relocate into the body of her cat led often to the stake or the gallows.

★

There's a case for saying that the credit for cats becoming true, unambiguous pets with no economic justification should be handed to weasels, for both the Romans and the Greeks used weasels and other mustelids for pest control. Cats were now free to be adored for their own sakes. They haven't looked back since. And they certainly haven't looked into our eyes with dog-like devotion.

This is a chapter about domestication. But cats are barely domesticated, unless domestication merely means living inside the *domos* – a definition that would encompass the swifts living inside ventilation shafts, the cockroaches scuttling over the kitchen floor, the weevils eating our books and the microorganisms living under the toilet seat and comprising a good part of the ecosystem we call *us*.

Cats aren't even in the *domos* for much of the time. They're out hunting, sleeping in flower beds and on warm walls, and drinking milk left out for them by some other *domos*.[28] When they are in your home, do they regard it as theirs? They regard it as a place where they can find food and shelter, but is that really any different from a lion seeing a waterhole as a place to drink and to harvest wildebeest? Cats haven't surrendered much of themselves, as dogs have. They are not part of us. When a cat owner dies the cat will be momentarily discombobulated before it finds another source of calories. A dog will feel that it has lost a leg and may pine forever.

⋆

We bring many other species into our houses: rats, mice, hamsters, guinea pigs, tortoises, snakes, spiders, insects and birds. But (with the possible exception of some unusually cognitively adept birds) we don't truly domesticate them. We might think of them as pets, but they don't think of themselves that way. Pet-ishness, for most species, is a unilateral business. A pet is a thing *we* have in the house for *our* entertainment or comfort. Pet-ishness, for most species, involves a wild, self-contained animal simply changing address but hanging onto its self-containment.

The history of the address-changes tells us some useful things about the main subject of this book: what sort of animals are we, who have such animals, on such terms, in our homes?

Take rats, for instance. As we, in our hunter–gatherer days, ate the scraps left by bigger, fiercer animals, rats watched hungrily and darted in to finish the bits we missed. We have always despised them as creatures of the shadows. When we started to farm, we resented them taking their share of our grain, and no doubt enjoyed seeing dogs and cats take revenge – a recreation organized sporadically over the centuries, and turned into a veritable industry in nineteenth-century Europe, when rat-baiting (where dogs competed with one another to kill rats released into a pit, and the spectators gambled on the outcome), was a mainstay of working-class culture.

Fancy rat breeding – probably using our familiar brown rat, *Rattus norvegicus*, as the substrate, was first recorded in Japan in the Edo Period (1603–1868), though it may have started even earlier in China. Trained rats (probably black rats, *Rattus rattus*) were displayed in Paris in 1667, but pet rats did not become common in homes until the nineteenth century. Thereafter, perhaps curiously and perhaps not, they became a marker of aristocratic, artistic and freethinking households, and were beloved of Ernest Hemingway, Mark Twain, Theodore Roosevelt and Beatrix Potter, amongst many others.[29]

⋆

Mice, again familiar from the very start of our history, and doubtless eaten enthusiastically by our ancestors, became particularly close neighbours when we became farmers. They are first mentioned as pets in the oldest Chinese dictionary we have – the *Erya*, dating from 1100 BCE, but most of whose entries probably date back to the third century BCE.

Specially bred fancy mice, like specially bred fancy rats, were a Japanese innovation, and were introduced from Japan to Europe in the early seventeenth century. They never became fashion accessories as did rats: mice are less charismatic and smart, can't be taught tricks, and don't elicit a gratifying shock from visitors. Rats, seen as wilder yet more tameable (there's an illuminating combination) and interactive, are more popular, or at least more cool. Mice are more inert, give less of themselves, and have never, outside the esoteric world of fancy mouse breeding (which is more like farming than pet-keeping) been *adult* pets. They tend to languish passively in small cages in children's bedrooms.

As do hamsters. Their dreary, uneventful lives in our homes contrast dramatically with their exotic origins in Syria and Turkey (most pet hamsters are Syrian hamsters), and with the adventure of their initiation to pethood. That initiation was the result of a 1930 expedition to the mountains around Aleppo by a Jerusalem-based biologist, Israel Aharoni, whose main interest was giving Hebrew names to the animals of the Holy Land. He had heard about a small furry animal called, in Arabic, 'Mr Saddlebags', and was determined to find and name it.

It proved elusive, but eventually, 8 feet down in a field of green wheat, he found a nest containing a mother and ten young pups (as they are called). He took them triumphantly away, but the stressed mother started to eat her own offspring. Aharoni killed the mother and, with great difficulty, hand-reared the survivors. They are the ancestors of the hamsters ignored by our children.

Guinea pigs have a still more colourful history, and a similarly dull present. They are Andean animals, perhaps domesticated (in the loose sense) for food 7,000 years ago. Sometimes they have been worshipped (for instance by the Moche of northern Peru in the early first millennium CE). They were sacrificed by the Incas, used in Peruvian medicine (black guinea pigs are said to be useful in diagnosis), and were imported to Europe by Spanish adventurers from the sixteenth century. In Europe they were never eaten in large numbers, but treasured as expensive curiosities. Queen Elizabeth I was fond of them, and they have been increasingly popular pets ever since.

★

Falconry's origins are obscure and contentious. It may have been pioneered in China, Manchuria, Central Asia, Iran or Mesopotamia 4,000 years ago.[30] Hard-to-date petroglyphs from the Teymaraeh region of northern Iran (from somewhere in the period 7000–2000 BCE) show a man on horseback with a raptor on his hand.[31] A pottery shard from Tell Chuera, in northern Syria, dated *c.* 3000 BCE, may depict a hunter carrying a bird of prey.[32] There are increasingly unambiguous depictions of falconry from Hittite sites from 2000 BCE to 1300 BCE. Once imported from the Middle East, it became a passion for mediaeval European aristocrats.[33]

A falconer with a bird on the glove is a chimaera. The bird takes on human qualities: it lives in a house; it keeps human hours; when hooded it relies on human eyes to know when there is prey worth hunting. The bird gives the human power to transcend many of our lumpen limitations; lengthens the human arm so that it can reach into the sky and snatch sand grouse; gives clairvoyant eyes that can see and kill a hare over the other side of the hill; turns our fingers to talons. No wonder birds of prey became potent markers of human status.

If we can't ourselves climb into the sky, courtesy of our peregrine, we often try to bring the heavens down into our kitchens and bedrooms. In his *Natural History*, Pliny the Elder wrote that aviaries 'were first set up by Marcus Laenius Strabo of the Order of Knighthood at Brindisi. From him began our practice of imprisoning within bars living creatures to which Nature had assigned the open sky.'[34] It was not so: the Sumerians had a word for birdcage, the fifth-century BCE Greek physician Ctesias expressed his amazement at the ability of some captive birds to speak human languages, and Nearchus and Onesicritus, Alexander's generals, collected Indian parakeets in 327 BCE and shipped them back to Greece in iron cages.

Soldiers and sailors of all ages brought birds, reptiles, primates and other exotica back with them to charm the ladies, and native birds too have often been incarcerated for their songs, their company, and for other reasons we will explore.

★

Modern owners of geckos, pythons and tarantulas might think of themselves as outlandish, but compared to the great pet-owners of old they are themselves tame. Two badgers follow the artist Giovanni Bazzi (Il Sodoma) in a 1502 fresco (PLATE 9). They were just part of his menagerie, which included squirrels, apes, marmosets, dwarf asses, tiny horses, jays, dwarf fowls, turtle doves and other animals, and enraged with their noise the long-suffering residents of Siena.

Shelley, who visited Byron in Italy in 1821, observed that

> Lord B's establishment consists, besides servants, of ten horses, eight enormous dogs, three monkeys, five cats, an eagle, a crow, and a falcon; and all these, excepts the horses, walk about the house, which every now and then resounds with their unarbitrated quarrels.... After I have sealed my letter, I find that my enumeration of the animals in this Circean Palace was defective, and that in a material point. I have just met on the grand staircase five peacocks, two guinea hens, and an Egyptian crane.[35]

★

Pliny's complaint about incarcerating birds (which sounds very contemporary), and Il Sodoma's and Byron's exuberant zoologizing, all point to a desire to make our homes continuous with the wild world – even if it means suffering and frustration on the part of an animal. We remake our homes to fit the animals, installing cat flaps and buying dog beds. And we remake our animals to fit our homes. Mere domestication isn't enough for us. We're not satisfied with pulling the wolf's teeth so that they don't sink into our buttocks: we've embarked on an elaborate project of cosmetic dentistry.

The dogs bounding through Egyptian tombs, up Mesopotamian pillars and across ancient Greek vases – dogs buried by Vesuvian ash and which serve as badges of aristocracy in Renaissance paintings – all look like dogs. They have deep chests, lungs good enough for chasing deer through Peloponnesian woods or gazelles across deserts, and long, sharp noses. Their bellies slope steeply to rippling back legs, and their front legs are ramrod straight. They are like gracile wolves with buzz cuts. They were often adored: their images sat on palace shelves and domestic mantlepieces, swung on thongs round necks, and went into their masters' and mistresses' graves. They may have been small, but were never cute. They were both elegant and useful – showing that we do not have to choose between function and beauty. They didn't wheeze or cough, their eyes didn't bulge, and they didn't get premature arthritis or have congenital heart disease.

There are still dogs like this: greyhounds, whippets and lurchers among them. And other dogs, such as German shepherds, look very like wolves. But wolfy dogs – indeed *doggy* dogs – are the exception.

As we've squashed our lives from the hills, the woods and the fields into the breeze-block filing cabinets we call our homes, we have made our pets smaller and less mobile. Dog bodies shrank with dog brains, keeping step with our own shrinking brains. We've got more manageable dogs now: dogs that puff as much as we do on their and our short daily waddle round the block: dogs that cope without chasing rabbits. We like disabled dogs, for they don't shame us; don't call us to account; don't remind us of what we were and truly are and might yet be.

John Caius, writing in *De canibus Britannicis* (1570), mocks small dogs: 'These puppies the smaller they be, the more pleasure they prouoke, as more meete play fellowes for minsing mistrisses to beare in their bosoms, to keepe company withal in their chambers, to succour with sleepe in bed, and nourishe with meate at bourde, to lay in their lappes, and licke their lippes as they ryde in their waggons.'

It's not *necessarily* dysfunctional to be small. Small dogs can still be dogs. But dogs like those described by Caius could still walk. What would Caius have made of modern 'teacup dogs', weighing less than 5 lb, bred from runts that in former generations would have been knocked on the head, designed (yes, *designed*) to live in a handbag colour-matched with their hair (or perhaps with their hair dyed to match the colour of their owner's gown, as was the dog belonging to Cora Pearl, a Parisian courtesan[36]), with kneecaps which would dislocate if the 'dog' tried to scamper across the Persian carpet, and advertised as never needing any outdoor exercise? Simon Garfield, in his book *Dog's Best Friend,* observes: 'The question "What is wrong with these dogs?" is easier to answer than the question "What is wrong with these breeders and owners?"' Quite right. We'll return often to that much harder question.

Garfield suggests that the 1990s – when labradoodles, known first in the 1950s, became popular – ushered in the true era of the designer dog, and it is true that from then on there was crescendoing absurdity. Listen to Garfield's baroque roll call of post-1990 hybrids: labradoodle, cockapoo, yorkiepoo, springador, cockador, lhasapoo, frug, jack-shih-tzu, chorkie, pomimo, borkie, bolonoodle, pooton, maltipoo, maltichon, malteagle, chonzer, schnoodle. 'One meets some of these dogs on [Hampstead] Heath', he writes, 'and they are irresistible, primarily because so many resemble stuffed toys.' But humans had moulded dogs extravagantly for a while before that. In an English print, dated 1867, a passer-by comments on a boy's dog:

> 'That's an Extraordinary Looking Dog, my Boy. What do you Call him?' 'Fust of all,' replies the boy, 'he wer' a Grey'ound, Sir, an' 'is Name was "Fly," an' then they cut 'is Ears an' Tail off, an' Tail off, 'an made a Masti' Dog on 'im, an' now 'is Name's "Lion"!'

The print is entitled 'Nature and Art'. It's a protest against meddling with the natural order.[37]

That we meddle might mean that we've forgotten, or can't see, or choose to ignore what the natural order is. Or perhaps, despite our protestations, it's an expression of our assumption that we're at the apex of the pyramid of being, and pet animals are ours to be used; toys, decorations or self-affirmers – no different in principle from the cows which give enjoyable but unnecessary steaks. We're relying on the traditionally perverted misconstruction of the Genesis mandate to 'subdue' the non-human world. God, in that account, delegated his authority to us, and we've interpreted it as a delegation not of an onerous stewardship responsibility, but as mere licence. God did another thing in the second Genesis account of the creation: he made humans in his own image. We're bad theologians: we've conflated the two Genesis stories, and assumed we have a right to recreate the world in our own image, however unattractive that image might be. Isn't that the most plausible explanation for brachycephalic animals?

The archetypal brachycephalic dogs, with squashed faces and woeful respiratory and cardiac function (surely designer dogs if ever there were any) are Pekinese and Shih Tzu, bred originally in China. They may be very ancient. Shih Tzu were favourites in the Ming dynasty (1368–1644), and may be descendants of Pekinese. Dog misery and dysfunction track urbanization, supposed human sophistication and sedentary lifestyle.

A 2015 study examined what the human subjects looked for in their dogs.[38] There were clear preferences for humanoid characteristics (coloured irises and faces that seem to smile) and, especially, the characteristics of human infants, such as big, widely separated eyes. We want literal fur babies.

We also want dogs who look like us – and since we want fur babies, that might suggest that we see ourselves, at some level, as fur babies still.

Studies comparing photos of dogs with those of their owners show that people buying pure-bred dogs select dogs that 'at some level, look like them, both in terms of their facial features and their broader physical features (e.g., size, hair, and attractiveness)'.[39] That will not surprise anyone who has ever walked round a public park. Intriguingly, the effect does not seem to apply where non-purebreds are adopted.[40] But what psychological mechanisms govern the choice? It seems that we choose our dogs using the same mechanisms engaged in choosing a human mate – namely assortative mating.[41] Katrina Holland suggests that a 'person's choice of pet may be a representation of the owner's self and owners might project their self-identity onto their pets'.[42] We use animals to express our own personality and preferences. There appears to be a link between the way that dog owners define themselves and their choice of a particular breed. If an owner thinks that race and personal behaviour are important in defining their own sense of self, they are likely to think that the breed of dog they have is important too.[43]

We make dogs in our own physical and psychological image (and vice versa), and, since our modern image isn't very appealing, our dogs look and feel grim too. Horace Walpole in his crotchety old age, crippled by gout, chose small, dyspeptic dogs with debilitating illnesses. We are in our crotchety old age as a species, and we do the same.

'How much is that doggie in the window?', asks the old song. 'The one with the waggly tail.' The answer, for a modern maltipoo (likely to be exhibited on a website rather than in a pet-shop window), will run into thousands of pounds. The cost to the dog of looking like that is incalculable.

The British Veterinary Association strenuously discourages the ownership of brachycephalic dogs, noting that they have 'Anatomical defects of the upper airway causing breathing difficulties often associated with overheating, sleep apnoea, and regurgitation, e.g. Brachycephalic Obstructive Airway Syndrome', and often have eye problems (including their hair and their eyelashes scraping their corneas, and a picturesque tendency for their eyes to pop out of their shallow sockets). They are often unable to mate or give birth naturally (requiring caesarean section), have repeated skin infections and dental problems (including teeth which swing sideways, causing rampant gum disease). They often require regular veterinary attention and corrective surgery. There's an epidemic of obesity in the UK's dogs.[44]

Does this medical picture sound familiar? It should. It's a description of many of us. That, in part, is why we choose the dogs we do. If they are loveable, so, we think, are we.

If it's troubling that we opt for badly disabled dogs, what does the market for 'kangaroo cats', sometimes known as 'squittens', with wholly unusable forelegs, tell us about ourselves? What can we conclude about the psychology of eighteenth-century Japan from its mania for 'waltzing mice' – mice with a neurological disorder which made them run in circles, bobbing up and down with tilted heads? Why, since at least the sixteenth century, has there been a thriving market for 'tumbler' pigeons, who have an obscure nervous syndrome which makes them do backwards somersaults in flight? Modern dog owners sometimes pay for false testicles to be inserted into the scrotum of their castrated dog. What does that signify?

We will return at the end of the book to examine ourselves in the mirror held up to us by our pets. But now it is time to look at the part pets play at each stage of our lives.

THREE

Childhood and adolescence

Animals watched as *Homo sapiens* was born and grew up. As we have seen, they profoundly influenced our childhood and adolescence as a species, and if (which is by no means clear) we're adults now they influence our adulthood too.

This watching and influence are reflected in our individual lives. Pets appear – though men do not – in many august depictions of women in childbirth. In *Birth of the Virgin Mary*, by the seventeenth-century Spanish painter Bartolomé Esteban Murillo, a small white woolly dog, forepaw raised, looks adoringly towards the baby, and is so alluring that a winged cherub, distracted, leans down to pat the dog rather than stand or fly in awe. The same dog, it seems, watches the birth of John the Baptist, as painted by Murillo, though the dog here is less interesting to the attendant cherubs. In Jan van Eyck's *Birth of John the Baptist* in the Turin–Milan book of hours (PLATE 7), a dog gnaws a bone and a cat investigates a bowl on the floor by the bed. And of course animals crowd round for a look at the infant Jesus in the manger.

If animals appeared at such auspicious births, they were plainly regarded as normal birth attendants. In most cultures other than our own, children heard and saw animals as soon as they heard and saw their own mothers. Unless you were born in one of our anomalous modern hospitals, dogs probably rushed in to eat your afterbirth.

It is no wonder that small children relate intimately to animals. Perhaps they relate more intimately to animals than to humans. Adult humans, after all, are large, cognitively sophisticated and highly linguistic creatures, and children are not. Adults make an effort at baby talk, but, though it increases children's interest in what the adult is uttering, it is not true talk. Adult humans are visually tyrannized animals: their vision plays a hugely greater part in their understanding of the world than do their other senses. Have you noticed that when we understand something we say 'Ah, I *see*'? We more or less ignore the contribution from our other senses. We are rarely aware, unless we concentrate particularly hard, of what we are touching, and except in extreme situations we might as well not have noses.

It is not like that for very young humans. They use all their sensory modalities. They construe the cosmos using a much wider bandwidth than us. They soak up sensation through the whole of their skin; they pick up handfuls of earth, eat it, smell it, and smear it all over their faces. Children are, in this sense, much more like dogs than like us, for though dogs lead with their noses as we lead with our eyes, it is unlikely that natural selection would have let dogs ignore the other sensory inputs as we, who have achieved (or so we think) a degree of autonomy from the demands of natural selection, tend to do. Adults need years of arduous mindfulness training to enable them to pay attention in the way they did when they were infants. We have forgotten how to pay attention: babies and dogs have not.

And adults are so high off the ground. Their sensory receptors, most of which are buried in their heads, are a long way from the floor, where many of the really interesting things happen. The floor is usually a much more olfactory place than the vertiginously high altitudes at which our noses fly. Dogs' and children's faces are just next to the floor – at the same level as one another. Children have a dog's eye and nose view.

Humans, too, once they start moving, are quadrupeds, just like dogs. Only later, when they hoist themselves onto their zoologically aberrant hind legs, do they become bipedal – and hence arrogant and abstract and other things that dogs are not, abandoning for ever the dog's and the baby's perspective, and replacing it with the grand sweeping vistas that make us value maps over the things maps represent, and turn us colonial, and make us disdain 'lower animals' such as dogs and babies.

It's not surprising that human children feel solidarity with animals, take cuddly animals to bed with them and like to read books about talking animals. I doubt that very young children distinguish clearly between toy animals and pets. Nor, since they have forgotten less than we have about the ways of the universe, do older, wiser, more confident cultures than ours. In ancient Greece, for instance, the commonest word for pet was *athurma* – the word used also for a toy, a plaything or *anything that delights*. From earliest times we have played with and delighted in actual and artificial animals. The children of the Indus Valley civilization (3010–1500 BCE) blew bird-shaped whistles and played with toy monkeys that slid down a string, and Egyptian toys over millennia included dogs (*especially* dogs) cats, mice, frogs and birds modelled in clay or wood.

Perhaps the most eloquent toys are the wheeled animals. For they show that children wanted the animals to travel with them and share and perhaps palliate their experience, just as that proto-dog walked alongside the child in the darkness of the Chauvet cave; wanted to be umbilically tethered to them by the drawstring, making the animal and the child one. There are countless examples in the archaeological record. One of the earliest known, and one of the most moving, is from the city of Khafajah in Iraq, and is dated to 2900–2330 BCE. It is a fat cylinder of baked clay with, at the front, above the hole for the string, the head of a sheep or goat, its eyes looking straight forward, sharing the child's view of the world into which they were both travelling. I'm sure its owner talked to it – long before the child had adult words – and believed that it talked back. Our conversations with our childhood animals, real and toy, are perhaps the most uninhibited, intimate and formative we will ever have. Perhaps our adult relationships are so frustrating because they lack the candour and reciprocity of the early wordless – or at least ungrammatical and unsyntactical – conversations with those animals.

It is in conversation with others that we learn what we ourselves are: that we recognize and refine the first-person sense we call consciousness. The novelist Edith Wharton wrote that her relationship with her first dog, Foxy, made her a 'conscious, sentient person'.[1] Catastrophic though its consequences might have been, it was the first recorded conversation between an animal (the serpent) and a human that led to the eating of the fruit of the tree of knowledge and evil, and directly to the self-knowledge that showed the first humans they were naked.[2]

In all cultures and all ages, talking animals have told us about ourselves, from Anubis (whom, if the Egyptians were right, we will meet for better or worse in the afterlife) via Aesop, Hans Christian Andersen, *Alice in Wonderland*, Beatrix Potter, Alison Uttley, *The Jungle Book*, to *Animal Farm*, Dr Seuss, Narnia, *The Magic Roundabout*, and Philip Pullman's daemons. Nowadays, fictional animals are being supplanted by other avatars. It will be interesting and scary to see (probably on psychotherapists' couches in several centuries' time) what effect this has on our self-knowledge and self-image.

For most of us, though, the first experiences of the great adventure of caring are likely to have been with toy animals. We feed, groom and sing to teddy bears before transferring our affections to humanoid dolls or, indeed, to real humans.

Some of us never transfer our affections from animal toys to 'real' things. Throughout John Betjeman's life his childhood bear, Archibald, was 'The only constant', though at the age of 9 Betjeman hid him in a loft, scared that his father would think him 'soft'. Musing in the poem 'Archibald', Betjeman acknowledges that some might think his own continued dependence on the bear denotes some deep-seated pathology, but cannot deny Archibald's enduring significance:

> And if an analyst one day
> Of school of Adler, Jung or Freud
> Should take this aged bear away,
> Then, oh my God, the dreadful void.

Though a Freudian analyst might seize the bear, I doubt a Jungian analyst would. Our governing Jungian archetypes are ancient, atavistic and zoological, and congenially represented by a toy bear in the bed.

We put animals on our children's plates, wallpaper, pyjamas and bedsheets, and apart from bears (something of an anomaly, resulting from shrewd commercial exploitation of Teddy Roosevelt's order for the euthanasia of a wounded bear in a Mississippi wood in 1902), the animals depicted are usually species commonly kept as pets – and dogs and cats in particular. It is so commonplace that we do not note the strangeness.

We, as adults, spend our lives valuing mortgages, riches and professional preferment, yet we value our children above all, and when we want to do right by them we surround them not with graphs of interest rates or icons of the boss we want to impress, but with pictures of cats. We apparently want our children to take their cues from the animals who accompanied us on our walk through evolution, rather than from the mores that rule our own lives. It's as if we delegate the most important part of our children's education to another species. We employ dogs, cats, hedgehogs and mice as moral wet nurses. And they do a very thorough job. Here is the author Jacky Colliss Harvey:

> As I look back, all the most important lessons of my life were taught to me by animals: the realities of love and loss and the impenetrability of death … the largeness of care and of responsibility. The effortless teaching of these lessons was, I am sure, why my parents believed that to have pets was a good, indeed essential, part of any childhood, expanding the imagination and sharpening empathy.… Growing up with animals rounds out your understanding of the world.… Animals are better educators, where sex is concerned, than any book … it was growing up with animals that made a liberal out of me. They also made me a thinking, pondering, question-asking being.… They were not me, but they made me think about myself. They made me study me.[3]

That is, or can be, the effect of pets. Perhaps, in our unreflective modernity, we don't explicitly buy pets for our children with those objectives. But it was not always so.

In many societies, interactions with animals are seen as ethical gyms, in which a child's good moral instincts can be strengthened by diligent working out. Better to get one's ethics right in the relatively safe environment of pet ownership than to learn ethical behaviour in other arenas, where more harm can be done by the unpractised. For Christopher Smart, who celebrated the ownership of his cat Jeoffrey in *Jubilate Agno* (1763), Jeoffrey was 'an instrument for the children to learn benevolence on'.

This view was not merely the intuition of an earnest and sentimental poet: it had the highest ecclesiastical warrant. Thomas

Aquinas declared that pity towards animals could provoke pity towards humans.[4] In a late-fourteenth-century *exemplum*, a little girl, being brought up as a nun, is taught that she must love Christ. But that, it is recognized, is a high and hard calling. She should work up to it gradually, and the best way is to start by loving her abbess's dog and bird.[5] Many a modern parent similarly hopes that care for a hamster will transmute into care for a little sister.

This ethic was hugely influential in the child-rearing policies of nineteenth-century evangelical America. It coincided with the thriving pet market of that century, and no doubt boosted it. Pets were seen as furry or feathered sermons. But the content of the sermons varied.

Often the gist was, as it had been for the young nun: practise kindness on animals, so that you can be kind to humans (where kindness *really* matters). Make the young responsible for the welfare of their pets, urged Lydia H. Sigourney, in her 1838 *Letters to Mothers*, because 'The rudiments [of kindness] are best taught by the treatment of animals.'[6] But there were other inflections too. The fiery evangelical preacher Charles Grandison Finney taught that the relief of suffering was itself a moral duty and, since animals appeared to suffer, they, while not sharing our moral significance, demanded the attentions of good Christian children. Making your pet mouse comfortable, the argument went, discharged a moral duty and strengthened your ethical backbone.

A simple, popular and wrong reading of the ordinance in Genesis might imply that humans had absolute, unfettered dominion over the non-human world. Many US evangelicals still believe this, but it is plainly inconsistent not just with scripture, but with responsible – or at least kind – pet ownership. Increased ownership of pets by children might well be partly responsible for the rediscovery of, or re-emphasis on, the obligation of stewardship. Owning animals, wrote Harriet Beecher Stowe in 1896, was 'a sacred trust from our Heavenly Father'.[7] Pets were not only sermons, but powerful scriptural exegetes.

Pet ownership could even play a part in the redemption of the cosmos, argued the English evangelical Charlotte E.B. Tonna. Since animals had fallen from grace alongside Adam and Eve, being kind to one's pets helped to restore the relationship broken by the Fall, and hence accelerate the return to Eden.

Animals were sometimes seen as less fallen than humans. It was Eve, after all, who had bitten into the fatal fruit, and though an animal – the snake – had enticed her to do so, snakes were unusually evil. One should not (said some) judge all animals by reference to the snake of Eden: 'the serpent was more cunning than all the wild animals the Lord God made on the earth', Genesis asserts,[8] and is specially anathematized: 'you are cursed more than all cattle, and more than all the wild animals of the earth', God told the snake.[9] There was a long and honourable Judaeo-Christian tradition of drawing (cautious) ethical lessons from the created order. That included pets. Pets, in their relatively unfallen innocence, might teach children how to live.

Dogs were commonly seen as examples of fidelity.[10] Be like a dog, and you would be a better human. Even cats could be moral models. An English child's handwritten text of uncertain date, but possibly late nineteenth century, records that 'Baby loves to run after [Pussy] … Pussy runs away because she does not like having her tail pulled or her eyes poked at.… Let us kiss this nice Pussy because she never scratches but is so good to Baby.'[11] Children, urges the child author, should be as forbearing as cats.

There is some scientific support for this view of the moral and psychological value of pet ownership. A 2021 study noted that

> Prior research has demonstrated that pet ownership is associated with physical, psychological, and social benefits among children. In particular, pets may play a role in the social-emotional development of children, such as in the development of self-esteem, autonomy, and empathy for others. Attachment to a pet may impact emotional development. A positive relationship between emotional bonds with pets and youth social-emotional outcomes has been reported.[12]

★

Pets teach us not only how to live, but how to die. The short lifespan of most pets means that children in pet-owning households meet death early and often, are forced to contemplate it, and learn that disembodiment is part of the deal of embodiment. They look into the patient eyes of their dying pets and (it may be thought) learn how to die with fortitude themselves. Their pets' deaths make children reflective and liturgical. Even the most flippant, secular child sheds tears over the dead cat, wonders where the cat has gone and whether she will join the cat one day, and leaves the iPhone for a moment to dig a hole in the garden, place the corpse reverently inside, and mutter a prayer. She will see the grave as forever sacred. Dead pets sacralize children.

Karen in the BBC sitcom *Outnumbered* buries a mouse, intoning solemnly over its grave:

> Brethren, we are gathered here in the bosom of Jesus to say goodbye to this mouse, killed before its time. We have given it bread and cheese for its journey to heaven, or at least if it goes to hell it will have cheese on toast.... Dust to dust, for richer or for poorer, in sickness or in health, may the Force be with you, because you're worth it. Amen and out.

On the cardboard cross marking the grave is written 'Mouse. Died 2008. Killed by mummy.'

Childhood pets were theologized in other, more subtle, ways. 'Do unto others as you would have them do to you', Jesus had taught, and for nineteenth-century children the 'others' often included the household animals. Pets were sub-people upon which (or upon *whom*) children should practise until they got their ethics right, and then, having graduated from the school of pet ownership, they could enter human society. This message was sometimes secularized: pets were useful as tutors of reciprocal altruism. If you scratched your dog's back, he, metaphorically, would scratch yours. Hence Sarah Josepha Hale's 'Mary's Lamb' (1830), a massively popular children's poem, in which a girl's love for her pet lamb incited the lamb to loyalty and love in return.[13] Part of this project was the generation of empathy. You would like to be understood yourself, the message was: so work at *understanding*. It was good for a child to think her way into an animal's world: it would dilute her selfishness and help her to feel and respond to the suffering of others. A ubiquitous image in nineteenth-century advertising was 'Can't you talk?', by the British artist George Augustus Holmes, in which a toddler, on hands and knees, gazes quizzically into the face of a collie, who gazes back with a similar expression (PLATE 26). The dog and the child each seem to be asking the question of the other.

In *Master Henry's Rabbit,* published in the United States in 1840, Henry forgets to feed his pet rabbit, and is sent to bed without his supper so that he can learn how the rabbit feels;[14] and in a more famous American novel of a similar era, Louisa May Alcott's *Little Women* (1868/69), Beth, usually a model child, does not feed her canary, and it dies.[15]

The moral point is clear: we should try to inhabit others' worlds.

Pets, then, were seen as potent moral transformers; preachers; exemplars of Christian values. And, of course, since they were so potent, the devil energetically sought to corrupt the relationship between children and their pets. In the mid-eighteenth century, Hogarth's *The Four Stages of Cruelty* (1750–51) had shown where you ended up if you mistreated animals. Tom Nero's apprenticeship in degradation progressed from hanging cats to being hanged himself.

Over the other side of the Atlantic, Lydia Maria Child's bestseller, *The American Frugal Housewife*, emphasized the parent's role in preventing the diabolic subversion of pet ownership.[16] She tells us of a mother who laughs as her toddler pulls a kitten's tail, but then beats the kitten when it scratches the child. The child, watching, is on the road to becoming a moral monster. He will tyrannize animals as a child, humans as an adult and, we are sure, share Tom Nero's fate. Treating an animal well, on the other hand, can turn Tom Nero into Tom Hero.

Such high-minded motives may form part of the thinking of at least some of us when we go to the pet shop and surrender to the demands for a hamster. But our motives are rarely pure and never simple. We know that we will end up doing most of the pet care: we will clean out the hamster, walk the dog and pick grass for the guinea pig on the way home from work. And we will certainly pay for it all.

We will ask later why we adults have pets we acknowledge as ours. But the fact is that our children's pets are, for most of the time, and for most practical purposes, ours too – though we continue to insist that the hamster is our daughter's and the rabbit our son's. What is going on? Perhaps there are four main reasons.

First, and least interestingly, adopting our children's pets lets us recruit those pets for all the purposes for which we have our own, grown-up pets.

Second, our children's pets remind us of our own childhood, which, if it was happy, we were and are loath to leave, and they are a respectable route back to it. They make it all right to be a crawling quadruped again – the state in which we were happiest, and which mentally we have never fully left.

Third, when we are down there on the floor, we are at the level both of the dog and of our own children. That alienating space between our children's eye level and our own adult standing eye level is abolished when we roll around with the dog. We meet our children down there in a way that is otherwise difficult or embarrassing. Animals create unique spaces in which to be with our children, and to be children.

And fourth, not only do those pets, and the crawling they entail, remind us of our own childhoods: they remind us of the childhood of our species. They bind us to our descendants and our ancestors. Those food, grooming, kennelling and veterinary bills are the price of time travel; the fees for a séance; the cost of atavistic self-realization.

I doubt those straplines will ever catch on with the advertisers.

★

Why do we choose for our children and ourselves the species we do? Why dogs rather than (for most of us) magpies, or guinea pigs instead of stoats?

We have seen some of the reasons already. Some are biological, and to do with (for instance) the advantage to the animal in entering into a coalition with us, or with the animal's intrinsic tameability. Some reasons are historical: we have guinea pigs in our homes partly at least because they were eaten and revered in the Andes and taken to Europe as curiosities by the Conquistadors. And some reasons are found in habit and tradition, together with the economic forces that support those habits and traditions. If there is an established tradition of dog ownership and a convenient infrastructure to help maintain it, dog ownership is likely to be more appealing than stick insect ownership.

But surely this is not the whole story. Stick insects are readily available and are cheaper and less demanding than dogs. Why, then, is there not a multi-billion dollar stick insect industry?

There are many strands to the answer. Stick insects are inadequate moral and theological tutors, and less good at reminding us of our origins and so what we really are, and less good at helping us to discover what our children are really like before it is too late. But the overarching reason is that we cannot relate meaningfully to stick insects, or even pretend that we can. It's a recognition that relationality is everything; is the web and the weave of the cosmos.

⋆

There comes a time when the pull of hormonal tides strain, sometimes to the point of dislocation, the relations between parent and child. Adolescence involves a declaration of independence by the child, and often a change in the child's relationship with pet animals.

The family dog, previously an icon of home, fireside and stability, may itself acquire a new lease of life as the companion in frontier-breaking adventures. As William Brown, the 11-year-old anarchic protagonist of Richmal Crompton's *Just William* stories, accelerated towards puberty, his scruffy dog, Jumble, along with his friends, the Outlaws, was his co-conspirator, helping William to outrage his parents and the norms of suburban society.

Dogs accompanied Victorian schoolboys on shooting and bird-nesting expeditions, and Victorian schoolgirls on sketching trips, wildflower collecting outings and sedate country walks. The dogs' function here was to represent the safety of the *domos*: to make it stretch to the countryside: to refashion the geography of the home just as the children's sex hormones were re-shaping the geography of their selves. And perhaps, too, because the *real* world outside the home is true wilderness, and so can be explored only in the company of a wild thing.

As any parent of teenagers knows, teenagers don't talk to their parents. Eventually they may acquire a language for doing so, but in the no-man's land between childhood and adulthood, teens have, at least for their parents, only grunting monosyllables, and for their peers mainly emojis. This, for human teenagers – who remain relational creatures – is painful and dangerous, and here the childhood pets (who, unlike their parents, don't ask for coherent sentences) can help. Dogs and cats seem to be loved and cuddled far more by teenagers than by children or adults. The teenager, in cuddling the dog, may be saying that she does not want to let go of her childhood, but she is saying too that the dog understands and comforts, non-judgementally, as her parents can't or won't.

All age groups say that one of the most important reasons for owning a pet is that it is 'something to talk to'. The vast majority (79 per cent in one study) of pet owners say that they talk continuously to their animals. The functions of confidant and partner are particularly important in the turbulent teenage years.

As the hormones rage, and the previously loved parents become increasingly tiresome, uncool and irrelevant, teenagers want (as do we all) to love and be loved. The current object of sexual infatuation is unlikely to fulfil the longing, but the impulse has to be dealt with. The pet does the job. Thomas Haynes Bayly, in his *Songs and Ballads* (1844), spoke for every dog-hugging adolescent: 'Some dog to follow, where'er I roam / Some bird to warble my welcome home / Some tame gazelle, or some gentle dove: / Something to love. Oh, something to love!'[17]

Perhaps this is the explanation for the change, at adolescence, in the preferences for particular types of animal. The teenage girl abandons her guinea pig and dotes instead on her horse or dog. Love of the sort mandated by surging hormones and alienation from one's parents requires an element of reciprocity. A horse nuzzles and responds to the reins. A dog wags its tail and licks your face. But guinea pigs are substitutes for neither parents nor lovers. In the courtly love literature of the Middle Ages, pets sometimes represent an absent lover. The modern over-cuddled dog may be fulfilling the same function.

The over-cuddling and the elaborate care teenagers give to their animals (in dramatic contrast to the care they don't give to their families or to themselves) may, speculates John Bradshaw,[18] have historically been a way for young women in particular to advertise their caring skills – and hence their marriageability. If a woman can look after a dog, a potential husband might think that she will be able to look after him and their putative children.

The same might go for men too. There's an intriguing study from France, in which a young man delivered an identical chat-up line to 240 young women he 'happened' to meet while out walking in public. He told them his name was Antoine, that he thought they were really pretty, and asked them for their phone number with a view to meeting up for a drink. When 'Antoine' was holding a dog on a lead, nearly a third of the women gave him their number. Dogless, his success rate was below 10 per cent. Adding 'with a dog' to a man's dating profile, even when the man expressly said that he was interested only in short-term relationships, nonetheless made some women think of him as a long-term partner.[19]

Dogs, it seems, are markers of reliability, loyalty and decency.

We're back to the theme we have already examined. The way we treat animals tells us (we instinctively think) something about how we treat humans. A boy who beats his dog might (we intuit) grow up to beat his wife and his children, and is best avoided. A boy who is kind to his dog is good husband material.

Is this instinct right? The picture is complicated. Many badger-baiting psychopaths are doubtless fond of and devoted to their pit bulls, but it would be unwise to regard that devotion as readily transferable to humans.

A summary of pet abuse statistics by the Humane Society of the United States notes a study in which 71 per cent of domestic violence victims stated that their abuser also targeted pets, and another which revealed that pet abuse had occurred in 88 per cent of families under supervision for physical abuse of children. Intentional abusers of animals were likely to be men under the age of 30 who hoarded animals (a practice with significant welfare consequences).[20]

What does seem clear – from a study of 500 sets of twins – is that a tendency to interact with animals, and, presumably, to enjoy that interaction, is more strongly determined by genetics than environment, and may therefore be more *constitutional*.[21] Of course it is hard to disentangle the contributions of genes and environment (children who have inherited animal-loving DNA from their parents are likely to grow up in households where they meet and learn to deal with animals), but nonetheless the DNA does seem to have the greatest say.

Whether a tendency to like animals is innate or not, taking care of animals involves many of the skills necessary for taking care of oneself, and is therefore good training for independence from the family. It's not hard to see why natural selection might have promoted teenage pet-devotion.

Whatever the reasons – evolutionary, emotional, psychological or whatever – for adolescent devotion to pets, pet animals accompany us into the liminal space between childhood and adulthood, keeping us company, perhaps providing some reassuring continuity with our childhood, while at the same time helping us to understand the new being that is erupting in us. Perhaps pets are good at this because they themselves occupy a similar liminal space all the time, being neither fully wild nor fully domesticated; often not fully animal but not fully human, though adopting many human habits and characteristics.

Barry Hines's *Kes* – the story of a disaffected boy, redeemed by his relationship with his pet kestrel, is the most detailed map of this space.[22] As it flew over the fields and woods of South Yorkshire, the boy, with the bird, could escape the dysfunctionality of the ground, and could grow into what he was.

For that sort of effect, you need a real animal. A mortal animal, sharing your vulnerabilities and fears, which inhabits the same world as you; which is, like you, a story moving through time from the beginning, via the middle, to the end; a story in which you can be a part. An animal with eyes that follow yours, and which both secretes its own oxytocin and stimulates you to secrete yours.

None of that is true of an important and rapidly expanding class of pets: virtual pets. Just as screens snatch children away from the world of real, embodied relationships, so virtual pets are increasingly ousting real, embodied animals.

It might be said that every toy is a virtual pet; a substitute for the real thing. But at least a teddy bear has a strokable body.

Why would anyone choose the virtual option? Let Steven Asarch make the case. He is a reviewer of the virtual pet market, who admits to having been addicted to his Digimon virtual pet for years.[23]

Dogs and cats, he reminds us, 'can be a lot of responsibility and may not be practical', but a virtual pet is 'always a viable option'. There is never any need to pay vet bills or 'clean up indoor accidents'. Most virtual pets are made of plastic or 'live inside an app on your smartphone', and need to be fed and cleaned 'just like a real animal'. Some beep when they are hungry or want to sleep, 'while others should be checked regularly to make sure they are feeling alright'. They are 'perfect for anyone age[d] eight and up. A child needs to be old enough to take care of it without dying' (presumably it is the pet, not the child, whose death is feared).

One high-rated pet is the 'Bitzee' ($24 on Amazon), which, using a hologram-type technology, makes it seem as if the pet is standing in 3D space. In fact 'it' is fifteen animals, each of which can be 'interacted with in unique ways, like petting them' or rocking them to sleep. As you play with your Bitzee its 'love meter' fills, 'allowing it to evolve from a baby into an adult and then eventually a super Bitzee, which adds … a treat that attracts another Bitzee' – like, I suppose, your charismatic dog being joined by others in the park.

Asarch's favourite budget pet is the Top Secret Toys Giga Pets Toy ($18) – again featuring a variety of species, including cats, dogs, unicorns, frogs, pixies, T-Rex, and 'cryptids' like Bigfoot, Nessie and Mothman. They, 'like most virtual pets … can be played with, fed, cleaned up after, cured when sick, and put to bed'.

Should you wish to specialize in dinosaur care, Asarch recommends the Tamagotchi Nano x Jurassic Park toy, which lets you hatch and care for twenty species of dinosaur.

But the 'crown jewel' of virtual pets is the Tamagotchi ($48), carried on your wrist like a watch. Its full colour screen allows you to 'brush, bathe and feed one of twenty pets'. They all have 'unique personalities that affect their personalities and behaviors'.

The Tamagotchi has a pedometer, so you can go for real walks with your pet, 'collecting items and crafting materials to make clothes to fit your style'. It has 'everything you need to form an attachment and connection with your new digital friend'.

These pets stand in a long and dishonourable tradition which can be traced back to the Pet Rock (rocks, sold for $4 each, complete with their own cardboard cage, lined with straw, and a manual entitled *The Care and Training of Your Pet Rock*) which, in 1975 and 1976, were marketed by advertising executive Gary Dahl. The idea came to Dahl as he listened to his friends moaning about their real pets. The combination of chutzpah, cynicism and satire was historic and extremely lucrative: Dahl quickly became a millionaire.

No doubt most rock owners were in on the joke, but others began to care for their rocks, lavishing on them love that would have been better directed elsewhere. Virtual pets, though conceived with Dahl's cynicism, seem to be taken entirely seriously by their owners, meeting our need to be wanted, to care and to be obliged. These are fine impulses in the abstract, but, if we have impulses only in the abstract, do we not un-make ourselves? Virtual pets are part of a wider and deeper project of disembodiment and dehumanization. Real, furry, feathered, scaly animals that require feeding with real food, and that make real mess, can help to arrest this project and mitigate some of its ills.

★

As we have seen, animal companionship was not thought by God to be sufficient for human thriving. That was why Eve was created.

Those human parents who buy pets for their children doubtless agree with God, and see pets as supplementing human companionship, training their children for better human relationships, and binding the children more tightly and functionally to the parents.

Are God and the parents right?

In a much-cited study involving 'insecurely attached' boys aged 7–12 years – boys who found it more difficult 'to accept social support from humans' – the effects on the boys' stress levels of a real dog, a toy dog and a friendly human were compared. Stress levels (as measured with salivary cortisol) fell significantly more when the boys interacted with the real dog than when they interacted either with the toy or with the human. The more the children stroked the dog, the more their stress dissipated.[24]

What should we conclude from this? Not, to be sure, that animals can take the place of human parents or functional human relationships. But our experience tells us that animals are healers; that they can reach parts of wounded humans that humans often cannot reach; that they can add materially to the warmth of a home.

It does no harm for parents to compete with the family pets for their children's devotion. Dogs, cats, fish, hamsters, guinea pigs, snakes and all: they should provoke us to raise our game. Which is the gist of what those old moralists were saying.

FOUR

Home, health and leisure

Home, in traditional families, is where the children are. Perhaps the previous chapter should have been much shorter, and said simply that we buy pets for our children because, for whatever reason, a house without animals is not a home.

Perhaps that is what those portrayals of animals at holy births are saying. Perhaps the animals are agents of a theological agenda, asserting that Jesus, the Virgin and the saints were born, like us, into real human families – for real human families include animals.

Although there are many depictions of the home in literature and the visual arts which do not involve household pets, there is no genre of such depictions from which animals are absent. Here is a reasonable generalization: if an author or artist wants to represent a happy home, they put an animal in the frame. Home is where we are ourselves, and where we are most ourselves (the stereotype goes) there pets will be. Most pets, after all, are archetypal domestic animals, and domesticity implies a *domos.*

The connection between pets and home is so close that where an ordinary home isn't possible, we may try to create it by importing animals. The double murderer Robert Stroud, the 'Birdman of Alcatraz', spent fifty-four of his seventy-three years in prison, forty-two of them in solitary confinement. The 300 canaries he kept in his cell made it more of a home.

Several friends lament that when their homesick children come home from university, they hug the dog and stroke the cat, but don't go near their parents. Animals define and delineate the home as the human inhabitants do not. Even if that does not happen, the home's animals are part of the family. Here is Maria Madan, a 17-year-old girl, writing in 1745 to her father, when he was serving in the army in Flanders. How best to remind him of home? By reminding him of his family. And what was the family? Maria was clear:

> *Inventory of our Family at Northill, 1745*
> Humans and servants, including laundry maid, house maid, nursery maid.
> Cattle: Popse, The Old Mare [yes, a cow], Little Cheltenham, The Colt.
> Dogs: Jenney, Turko.
> Puppies: Young Turko, Young Jeney, Sachine, Rover, Donna, Dido, Kanger, Marcia
> A sow, 10 piggs, a boar, a cat.
> 3 kittens, 2 guinea pigs, 2 guinea piglins, 2 geese, 6 French ducks, 6 English [presumably ducks], 10 chickens, 2 starlings, a black-bird, 2 gold-finches, a Green-finch, an ass, an ass-colt, an owl.
> In all 82.[1]

Pet ownership skyrocketed during the Covid pandemic (creating an epidemic of unwanted pets when the pandemic receded and people went back to work). The National Pet Owner Survey in the United States identified three major reasons for the increased ownership: first, that people were spending more time at home; second, 'my family wanted a pet' (more than they had previously wanted one); and third, 'I was home alone and wanted pet companionship.'[2] We will look at the third of those reasons later, but the first two overlapping reasons suggest that pet ownership is seen as defining or creating a home. If home is more home than it was because you spend more time in it, it needs to be made more homely by containing more animals.

We personalize our homes. We choose the house, and then the wallpaper, the carpets and the furniture, at least partly on the grounds that they express something of what we are. Just as a choice to insert prosthetic testicles into your castrated dog might express something of what you are, so might your choice of species. A study carried out by a pet-food manufacturer concluded that cat-owning women are gentle and submissive, men with big fierce dogs are compensating for their small genitals, bird owners are sociable and unpretentious, horsey men are aggressive and dominant, turtle keepers are reliable and hardworking, ferret owners careless, those who own snakes, spiders and other scary pets are unconventional, hedgehog enthusiasts are sloppy and unsympathetic, and rabbit keepers complex but relaxed.[3]

Most of us will recognize some truth in at least some of these stereotypes. Sometimes pets are chosen specifically to project a particular image. We all know people who own gun dogs but no guns, and whose unhappy, underexercised suburban dogs exist to declare that their owner, despite working all hours in an inner city office, is a countryman at heart. But no one chooses a ferret to assert that they are careless: the ferret is a covert marker of an unacknowledged trait. The ferret-owner confederation declares a fundamental characteristic more loudly than the owner's own mere carelessness. In images down the aeons dogs (in particular) are used to affirm and reinforce gender stereotypes. Tiny lapdogs announce feminine daintiness and domesticity; athletic hunting dogs lying by the fire at the master's feet say that the household is not his true domain – he is a hunter, and soon will be outdoors where he belongs, killing things.

Animals which serve no obvious function, but simply consume resources, are potent social markers because of their very uselessness. In a twelfth-century sermon, theologian Hugh of Saint Victor bellowed: 'Even though the ape is a most vile, filthy and detestable animal, clerics like to keep one in their houses and to display it in their windows, so as to impress the passing rabble with the glory of their possessions.' The same might be said of every coiffured toy dog at the feet or under the arm of a rich woman from the Middle Ages to contemporary Hollywood.

There's no reason to suppose that affluent households in, say, the Middle Ages, spent a smaller proportion of their income on pets for than we do now – and accordingly that the strength of the social signalling of pet keeping was any less then than now. The costs associated with an individual mediaeval animal may have been smaller: there were often hordes of them, economies of scale no doubt applied, and there were no vet bills or insurance premiums to pay. But the sheer numbers of mediaeval pets made them a significant expense.

That's not to say that humbler households didn't keep pets. They did. A register of households in New Romney, Kent, from the time of Elizabeth I suggests that every single household had a dog. An English statute of 1793 imposed a dog tax, and the returns show a dog population of around 1 million at a time when the human population was 6½ million. There was 'scarce a villager who has not his dog', it was said.[4] Daniel Defoe, in his *Journal of the Plague Year*, published in 1722, says that there were five or six cats for every London hearth.[5]

These animals in the homes of poorer families were no doubt not thought of as *just* pets. They were useful, to a degree, and, being foragers and scrap-eaters, were much cheaper per canine capita than the animals in the big houses. But did they really pay their way? It seems unlikely. They didn't cost *nothing*, and when the household income was practically nothing, taking on another financial burden demands a non-financial explanation.

Figures released by the UK Office for National Statistics show that expenditure in 2022 in the UK on pets and related products reached £9.89 million – a 182 per cent increase from 2005, when the figures began to be collected. That figure did not include veterinary and other pet-care services – which themselves totalled over £5.3 billion in 2022 (up from £1.1 billion in 2005). In 2022 the UK dog food market reached around £1.84 billion, closely followed by cat food, at £1.43 billion. The UK pet food industry's own statistics estimated that in 2024 the total UK pet food market was worth £4.1 billion. Respondents between the ages of 65 and 74 spent an average of £6.90 per week on pets and pet food. Dog insurance cost an average of £332 per year, and a total of £1 billion was paid out in claims under pet insurance policies.[6]

Putting it all together, owning a dog cost, on average, £1,875 a year – of which the largest proportion (£450) was the expense of boarding. Median household disposable income in the UK was £32,300 in the financial year ending 2022, and for the poorest fifth of the population it was £14,500.[7] For households in the median position, that dog represented nearly 6 per cent of the disposable income. For the poorer households it was almost 13 per cent.

There are endless ways to spend more of your income on your pet, and of course the pet industry harnesses your guilt to persuade you to do so. You will not be a good pet-parent, you're told, unless you do. 'It's not just about taste', one dog-food ad reminds us: 'this food also delivers all the nutrition your growing pup needs to thrive. With the perfect balance of protein, vitamins and minerals, this gourmet dog food is designed to promote healthy growth and development in your furry friend. So if you want to give your puppy the very best start in life, choose our Gourmet Chicken, Turkey and Salmon with

Country Veg Puppy Food.'[8] It's 'cooked gently to retain nutrients', it is 'ethically produced', the recipes are 'designed to aid gut health', are 'fully hypoallergenic' and contain no artificial flavourings or preservatives.

Being part of the family, pets should celebrate with us. Take Christmas, for instance. You might buy a 'Wufers Advent Calendar Cookies Box', with a hand-decorated cookie, made with yogurt-based frosting, behind each door, or 'Puppy Scoops Holiday Ice Cream', 'creamy, yet lactose-free', and available in hot carob, peanut butter cookie, Christmas cookie and roast beef flavours, or 'Claudia's Canine Bakery Gourmet Dog Treats', each 'designed to tantalize your dog's taste buds', many of which are 'artistically hand-decorated, adding a visual appeal that mirrors the joyful spirit of the Christmas season'. Zuke's Mini Natural Holiday Trees are 'crafted into charming tree shapes', while the addition of cranberries 'not only lends a festive touch but also provides antioxidants'. DreamBone Holiday Variety Vegetables and Chicken Dog Treats are also 'shaped like Christmas items, including snowmen, Christmas trees and gingerbread men', while Bocce's Bakery adds Figgy Pudding and Santa S'mores to its usual range for the festive season.

It could be worse, and it often is. In 2009 Thai jewellery designer Riwin Jirapolsek made a titanium tiara, coated with emeralds and diamonds, for his Maltese terrier. It was valued at $4.2 million. Then there is the 'Amour Amour' dog collar ($3.2 million), made from platinum, white gold, crocodile leather, and studded with 1,600 diamonds; Gucci's Radura pet bed ($7,500), whose luxurious cotton canvas upholstery is treated with stain repellent and an antibacterial agent; Roberto Cavalli's couture line for dogs, including silk shorts, satin-trimmed bathrobes and velour tracksuits; the Louis Vuitton Dog Carrier ($2,940), whose timeless charm is accentuated by the natural cowhide leather trim; the Royal Crown Derby 'Imari' pet bowl ($2,400), brushed with real gold; the Swarovski cat flap, encrusted with over 1,000 crystals ($1,220); and the Prada Nylon Dog Harness ($1,020), 'your furry friend's passport to the world of high-end fashion', whose side-release buckle ensures that 'practicality meets panache'.[9] There is jewellery designed specially to cover your cat's anus, and if you visit FerretShopKidsPets and are happy to part with €59.79, your ferret can wear a white princess dress.

Perhaps the world's most expensive modern kennel is the Hello Kitty Doghouse ($32,000 in 2007) encrusted with 7,600 crystal beads, and big enough for a Chihuahua or small terrier, but it looks tacky beside Marie Antoinette's *niche de chien* in the Metropolitan Museum of Art (PLATE 17), made of gilded beech and pine, lined with striped beige and blue silk, covered in velvet, and decorated with acanthus leaves, and both Hello Kitty and the *niche* would doubtless be eclipsed by the golden reliquary, lined with rare furs, inhabited by Petitcrieu, the lapdog (though half leopard) given to Isolde by Tristan.[10]

It is hard to know whether to laugh or cry. Certainly pet bling is an easy and satisfying target for satirists. 'Treat your pet to their first Le Creuset', urged a chalkboard outside an English kitchenware retailer.

The commonest response, though, is outraged denunciation. 'The wealthy provide for their dogs more readily than for the poor', screeched the fourteenth-century Dominican preacher John Bromyard, 'more abundantly and more delicately too.'[11] This, taught his near contemporary, Geoffroy de La Tour-Landry, was spiritually very dangerous. He described how a woman who overfed her dogs and neglected the poor got her comeuppance. On her deathbed, he wrote, 'there was an amazing sight, for two little black dogs were seen on her bed and as she was dying they licked her mouth, so that by the time she had died, her mouth was black as coal.'[12] Chaucer, though more restrained, plainly disapproves of the pet-keeping policy of the Prioress, Madame Eglentyne: 'Of smale houndes hadde she, that she fedde / With rosted flesh, or milk and wastel-breed.'[13]

The pamphleteer Jonas Hanway thundered, in 1756, using capitals to add disgust:

> We may sometimes see a fine lady act as if she thought the DOG, which happens to be under her precious care, is incomparably of more value, in her eyes, than a HUMAN creature… The costly chicken is ordered for the CAT or DOG, by her who never thinks of giving a morsel of bread to relieve the hunger of a MAN.[14]

He's got a point. Every four seconds a human dies of hunger.[15] One charity, Mary's Meals, estimates that school meals for a year for a child in the world's poorest countries cost £19.15.

If that doesn't convince, perhaps the argument from pet welfare will. There is a World Pet Obesity Awareness Day, and with good reason. Some 59 per cent of dogs and 65 per cent of cats in the United States, Canada and Europe are obese or overweight, with consequences akin to those of obesity in humans.[16] This is not a new concern: the thirteenth-century German polymath Albertus Magnus was lured away from Aristotle, alchemy and metaphysics into veterinary medicine, declaring that when rich ladies give their pets treats, the pets get stomach complaints. 'This is seen most often in the ladies' small dogs which almost always die of constipation. Let them be given oatmeal that has been steeped in warm water to the consistency of thick porridge. Or else let them be fed with leavened soft bread and let them be given a little milk whey and they will become loosened and become swift and whole.'[17]

Why the diamond-studded collars and jewelled kennels? Why the figgy pudding biscuits, the organic duck and the golden food bowl? Pet owners tell themselves that it is to express gratitude to the animal. Here is a typical advert, this time from a high-end clothing retailer, branching out, at the time of the Crufts dog show, into lush leads, luxurious collars and branded hedgehog toys:

> We thought what better time to celebrate that special canine in your life. Big or small, your pooch is always there for you, whether it's in the form of a personal trainer, getting you out and about, a comedian, making you laugh, or your therapist – they're such good listeners! Your best friend deserves a little pampering, so why not treat them to a new toy, smart new coat or stylish new collar![18]

Quite apart from any arguments about the ethics of resource allocation in a world of limited resources, and, in the case of food, any veterinary arguments, the obvious response to the question 'Why not treat them?' is that the animals themselves either couldn't care less, or, if they do, would prefer an old, smelly bed by the fire to a jewelled cage.

Who are the treats for? They are for the owners, pursuing a variety of psychological agendas, including the aim of making the dog look and live like us (even – or perhaps especially – when we live lives of wheezing, limping obesity) and for the people they want to impress. To think of the treats as for the dog allows guiltless self-indulgence.

There is something interesting here, though. If the treats are for the owner, yet the owner truly believes they are for the dog, then the owner and the dog seem to have become assimilated with one another. It's almost shamanic.

We choose constitutionally unfit animals, and make them unfitter. Yet we, and many headlines, insist that our pets make us healthier. They give us stronger hearts, we hear, reduce our triglyceride and cholesterol levels and our blood pressure, and make us live longer.

The connection between animals and human health has been asserted since antiquity. The Greek god of medicine, Asclepius, often had a dog at his heels. The Romans saw dogs as healers sent by the god

Mars, and the Celtic god Nodens, with a medical portfolio similar to that of Asclepius, was often accompanied by dogs.

John Bradshaw has analysed the studies. There is indeed a connection between heart health and dog ownership, but it is very hard to disentangle causation and correlation. Probably dogs help cardiac fitness because they get you off the sofa and walking. Simply being outside, particularly in woods and other green places, and simply being active, confer measurable health benefits. Your dog is probably just taking you to prophylactic and therapeutic places.

But animals – and particularly dogs and cats – do make us calmer. Just looking at videos of animals (ducks, kittens, cats, puppies, dogs, alpacas, tiger cubs, lion cubs, baby gorillas, monkeys and quokkas) caused stressed students and university staff to feel better. Their blood pressure, heart rates and anxiety levels plummeted.[19] In another study, just ten minutes of interaction with dogs and cats caused significant reductions in levels of the stress hormone cortisol.[20] Military veterans with a diagnosis of PTSD who owned a service dog reported significantly lower levels of anxiety, anger, sleep disturbance and alcohol abuse compared to dogless veterans with a similar diagnosis.[21]

Over 7,000 dogs are registered to Amazon HQ in Seattle, and about 800 come each day. They're regarded as stress-busting, mood-enhancing, productivity boosters. There are dog treats at reception, dog drinking fountains throughout the building, and a 'doggie deck' (whatever that is) with a fake fire hydrant (No, I didn't understand the particular appeal of a fire hydrant either).[22] Amazon's "Woof Pack" manager says that the company has been dog-friendly 'since Day 1'. 'Having dogs in our workplace is an amazing treat. They make employees smile, and we're proud this is such a uniquely Amazonian tradition. It's truly ingrained in our company culture.' Amazon dogs, reported the *LA Times*, 'can stop to lunch on flank steak or New Zealand venison purchased by their owners at a newly opened branch of Just Food for Dogs, an Irvine-based chain offering "human-grade" meals. They can eat cream-filled cannolis [*sic*] from Puddles Barkery [*sic*]. Some have their own Instagram accounts.... When their owners have meetings, dogs can pop into a doggy day-care spot for a shampoo, blow dry and "nail pawlish".'

Dogs reduce the agitation of dementia patients, diminish depression and enhance mood, help to broker conversation between children with autism-spectrum disorders and their therapists and friends, cause the outpouring of oxytocin we've seen already, and alleviate loneliness. Since loneliness is deadly – associated with suicide, depression, heart disease and alcoholism – our dogs may indeed save us. Cats seem to have similar effects.[23] Bob, the stray cat rescued by James Bowen in *A Street Cat Named Bob*,[24] ended up rescuing Bowen, helping to wean him off heroin and then methadone. The cat 'is what I wake up for every day now. He's definitely given me the right direction to live my life.'[25]

Olive Thorne Miller, writing in 1894, anticipated fairly accurately the current scientific consensus:

> The use of the pet as an aid to health has not been considered as it deserves. No instinct is truer than that of the unmarried woman of lonely life to surround herself with pets. The companionship of cats and birds in solitary lives has unquestionably kept more people than we suspect out of the insane asylum; and if friendless men took kindly to them, there would be fewer misers, drunkards, and criminals than there are now. It seems to be the divinely appointed mission of our furred and feathered friends, who never grow gloomy with care, never suffer from envy, ambition, or any of our soul-destroying vices, to make us forget our worries, to inspire us with hope, and thence with health.[26]

William Cowper's dog, Beau, was a powerful antidepressant. Cowper's biographer says of Beau: 'Whether frisking amid the flags and rushes, or pursuing the swallows when his master walked abroad, or whether licking his hand or nibbling the end of his pen when in his lap at home, Beau ofttimes, like his predecessor, the hare [Cowper kept three pet hares too], beguiled Cowper's heart of thoughts that made it ache, and forced him to a smile.'[27] Laure Desvernays, in 1913, understood: 'The caressing regard of a dog, the sweet touch of a cat, the rhythmic modulations of a bird in a cage, the triumphant trills of a canary, have they not, on occasion, chased away our melancholic thoughts?'[28]

These old insights are creeping slowly into the contemporary mainstream. There are many schemes for animal (and particularly dog) visits to hospitals, health centres and care homes. The visits are often warmly appreciated, though their therapeutic benefits are difficult to evaluate. My own college has a much loved college cat, Walter, who is most avidly hugged and stroked during exam time (PLATE 40). Companies loaning stress-busting animals like alpacas to university institutions in the exam seasons do brisk business, and the reports make happy reading – except, apparently, for some of the animals, which soak up so much stress that they may need psychotherapy themselves.

As those sultry teenagers know, we talk to animals as we will not talk to humans. Animals aren't judgemental. They don't criticize our weaknesses. It's not embarrassing to cry in front of the cat. And the conversation with an animal – precisely because it is not mediated by weaselly words, but by all the inchoate senses which engage our intuitions rather than our cognition, speaks from deep to deep, without posture, pretence or obfuscation. In some ways, then, we may relate more profoundly to our animals than to our humans, and our animals may be great tutors in the art of relationship more generally.

Not only do dogs help men get dates – marking them out as carers, and hence potential mates (remember Antoine?); they also signify (so our intuitions insist) general reliability. Bradshaw cites a study in which a disreputable-looking man walked along the street with and then without a disreputable-looking dog. He was eight times more likely to be smiled at or approached when he had the dog. Interestingly, when he and the dog were both well dressed, only 35 per cent more people engaged with him.[29] The dog, in short, seemed to demolish snobbery, presumption, class prejudice and inhibition. Other animals, too, may be a shortcut to human intimacy. Mark Twain, in a posthumous essay, wrote that 'When a man loves cats, I am his friend and comrade, without further introduction.'[30]

Dogs make it easier to live not only with others, but also with ourselves. And to live, moreover, in the present – the concrete – rather than in some past or future abstraction. There are two reasons. First, dogs are unlikely to be committed abstract thinkers. Their agendas are written by the appetite of the moment, and if we bond with them we will be forced into the moment too. And second, not only do dogs make us smile at other humans in the park; they make us talk to them in doggy ways. Another study cited by Bradshaw revealed that dog ownership, though it increased the number of smiles, did not increase the *number* of conversations. But it affected the content of the conversations that did happen. Those conversations, unsurprisingly (and whether the dog was present or not) centred on the dog and on how the dog was *now*.[31] It rooted the humans in the here and now. That's very rare: it's the goal of mindfulness meditation.

We only truly exist now, and so the dog-facilitated quest to live now is a quest to be more truly ourselves: a goal more likely to be realized in the home (or so we seem to think) than anywhere else.

We seek in our homes what the studies, the ancient dicta and the anecdotes say that animals can give us in the clinics, the temples and the workplaces. Animals help us to live healthily, happily, in the moment, and, by making our homes their homes, more securely.

★

Today, where benefit and detriment are rigorously audited, and every device, experience and animal star-rated on a review website, there is no shortage of advice about the type of pet to fit your lifestyle.

'Corydoras, also known as Cory Catfish, are endearing bottom-dwellers', Acquariumnexus.com, tells us.[32] They 'make an excellent addition to a beginner-friendly community tank, thanks to their amiable nature and unique appearance. These adorable little helpers enjoy sifting through the substrate for scraps, thus assisting in maintaining aquarium cleanliness. Keeping them in groups of six or more will deter potential shyness and allow their personalities to truly shine.'

The Kennel Club, the governing body for pedigree dogs in the UK, lists all the criteria a prospective dog owner should consider, including gender. Here, for instance, is the advice about grooming:

> It's worth considering how much grooming your preferred breed will need. If you have reservations about spending hours brushing your dog, then you may wish to consider a low-maintenance breed. Some short-muzzled breeds need regular cleaning of their skin folds to prevent infection, so they still require grooming despite their short coats. Other dog breeds may have a strong smell; some dribble a lot![33]

Consider this advice in the context of the maxim that dogs look like their owners. Perhaps they smell and dribble like them too.

Prudence is often trumped by love. We do not choose our human mates by assessing whether they have a critical mass of desirable characteristics, and it is no doubt right that we do not. Should we approach pet ownership differently?

Whether we should or shouldn't, a pet (barring fish, perhaps) who starts by being simply a compendium of qualities quickly acquires a name, and becomes not an animal, nor even *the* animal, but a friend, and a suburb of the owner's soul. 'If a man does not soon pass beyond the thought "By what shall this dog profit me?" into the large state of simple gladness to be with dog, he shall never know the very essence of that companionship which depends not on the points of dog, but on some strange and subtle mingling of mute spirits.' So wrote John Galsworthy, cutting to the quick in a 1912 essay.[34] We want our spirits to be mingled with something very different from us, and are prepared to pay a high price for it.

What does the mingling give us? Two things above all: peace and companionship.[35]

'To sit with a dog on a hillside on a glorious afternoon', wrote Milan Kundera, 'is to be back in Eden, where doing nothing was not glorious – it was peace.'[36] It's a revealing observation, as true for the fireside as for the hill. The home, in endless depictions, is Eden rebuilt: a place from which the serpents of commerce and busyness are excluded, and where we can be authentic, discarding the masks that the world outside compels us to wear. Yet the peace of this Eden – this perpetual Sabbath – is not only the absence of strife. It is a vibrant peace, vibrant with the purr of cats, the bustle of dogs and the whirr of hamster wheels. Eden was where the relationship between humans and animals was closest and happiest. It would not have been Eden without the animals.

The companionship of animals has often been criticized. It was implicitly criticized by God, who, as we have seen, decided that Adam's friendships with non-human animals weren't enough, and that for Adam to thrive properly he would need a human ally too.[37]

The love of an owner for an animal sometimes evokes jealousy. Why can't my beloved Lesbia love and fondle me as she does that sparrow? moaned Catullus:

Sparrow, my darling's delight,
whom she plays with, whom she holds in her lap,
to whose pecking beak she gives her fingertip
and teases to nip sharply,
whenever it pleases her, my radiant heart's desire,
to amuse herself with something beloved,
so that, I suppose, then her strong passion subsides,
and she has a little solace from her longing.
Would that I could play with you as she does,
and lighten the sad cares of my soul![38]

The criticism is often framed in terms of unnatural love. *Proper* humans, the argument goes, lavish affection on other humans, not animals.

It's an ancient and very modern trope. Plutarch, writing in the second century CE, recorded that the Emperor Augustus was disgusted by the sight of wealthy foreigners in Rome 'carrying up and down with them, in their arms and bosoms, young puppy dogs and monkeys, embracing and making much of them'. Augustus 'had occasion … to ask whether the women in their country were not used to bearing *children*'.[39]

Pope Francis, in 2022, said that 'Today … we see a form of selfishness. We see that some people do not want to have a child. Sometimes they have one, and that's it, but they have dogs and cats that take the place of children. This may make people laugh but it is a reality.' This, he added: 'is a denial of fatherhood and motherhood and diminishes us, takes away our humanity'.[40]

The Pope's comments were bitterly resented by pet owners, as no doubt the Emperor Augustus's were by some of those wealthy foreigners. Tracy, 43, who lives with her twelve rescue cats, and could not have children of her own, said that she was 'so angry about the Pope stating people are selfish for having pets instead of kids'. Her cats, she said, were her family. 'They make my day, every single day….

The fact I can look after them, love them, and keep them safe, is a huge privilege. I suffer with my mental health so my pets help me no end with unconditional love and give me a reason to keep going. I honestly think if I had no one to look after I wouldn't be here.'

Another owner, Emma, said that pets 'often provide a place for people who are looking for somewhere extra to put their love, but can't have, or don't want children.... Most human beings have a need to direct their energies positively towards others, whether that's humans or animals.... I think that responsibility and purpose is good for the human psyche: if you feel responsible for something you have a level of purpose, and when you have purpose, you have meaning, and life feels worthy.... Lots of us use animals that way, as we have this overflow of positive love and we don't want it to go to waste.'

James, who found himself single at the age of 40, 'didn't want to miss out on being a father, as I felt this is a relationship I wanted to have in my life.... So I made the big decision to get a dog and experience at least that sort of parental moment – after being a lifetime cat person. And now me and the dog are inseparable, and he's my life – just like a child.' His dog, Loki, is 'definitely not a "pet", but more a proper companion who I love spending all my time with – just like if I had a romantic partner in a long-term relationship.' It was a huge step at first, he said, 'with the potty training, all the other bits of training, sleep patterns, etc, it was like having a baby. There were lots of sleepless nights.'

'Animals always need you, whereas children won't', said a therapist involved in helping people navigate many of life's crises. 'Children change, animals don't – you always know what you are getting with a pet and taking care of them is very rewarding in so many ways. In a complex world full of complicated relationships that are often conditional, pets cut through that – and just love you unconditionally, every day.'[41] Freud would have agreed. Animals offer 'affection without ambivalence', he wrote, 'the simplicity of a life free from the almost unbearable conflicts of civilization, the beauty of an existence complete in itself; and yet, despite all divergence in the organic development, that feeling of an intimate affinity, of an undisputed solidarity'.[42] The tortured writer J.R. Ackerley realized, after spending most of his life in search of an ideal human friend, that the ideal was perhaps his dog, Queenie, who, unlike capricious humans, gave him 'constant, single-hearted incorruptible uncritical devotion which it is the nature of dogs to offer'.[43]

It is one thing to opt for a pet if one cannot, for whatever reason, have children. It is quite another not to have children because one thinks a pet preferable to a child. There is evidence that this is happening. James Serpell, a professor of ethics and animal welfare at the University of Pennsylvania, suggested (while noting that correlation is not causation) that pet keeping may be a factor in the reduced human birth rate seen in many countries, including the UK and the USA. He highlighted the language many pet owners use to talk about their pets – such as 'pet babies', and the appeal of anatomical features in pets that mimic those of human infants. 'These infantile or paedomorphic traits influence humans' perceptions of cuteness as well as eliciting caregiving motivations and behaviours.' He pointed to brain imaging studies showing that this tendency is 'relatively hard-wired in the brain', and localized to the medial orbitofrontal cortex. Both in the UK and the USA, human birth rates are inversely proportional to the rates of pet keeping. Dogs and cats increasingly occupy our medial orbitofrontal cortex, and may be elbowing babies out of it.[44]

Augustus and the Pope gave rather different reasons for their suspicion of pets, but perhaps behind the reasons of each was an instinct that biological boundaries between species are ethically fundamental – an instinct reflected in the lines drawn between the various creatures in the early chapters of Genesis, and the distaste for human–animal chimaeras.

Both Augustus and the Pope would be horrified by the breach of those boundaries in modern bedrooms. Not sexually, but companionably. A survey of US pet owners found that 62 per cent of small dogs, 41 per cent of medium-sized dogs and 32 per cent of large dogs sleep with their owners; that 62 per cent of cats sleep with their adult owners; and another 13 per cent of cats sleep with children.[45] And while 47 per cent of respondents to a survey by the American Animal Hospital Association would opt for a human companion if stranded on a desert island, 50 per cent would take a dog or cat instead.[46]

The desert island figures are unsurprising, given the other views of pet owners. While 30 per cent thought that their spouse or significant human other listened to them best, 45 per cent thought their pet was the best listener.[47] More than half said it was very likely that they would risk their life for their pet. Even if these attitudes are not in themselves pathological, they can lead to undoubted pathology.

Bradshaw cites Leonard Simon, a psychoanalyst who practised in New York in the 1980s, and who interviewed hundreds of randomly selected pet owners. Simon said that

> Not everything I heard was benign. With some people I became convinced that their lives would have gone altogether differently – and probably better – if there had been no pet. All too often I heard of wasted years and stagnant lives in which almost everything a person did revolved around his animal. I heard of divorces that might never have happened and I heard of some that probably should have happened long before and [after the pet died] they finally did. I heard of children that were neglected for the sake of a pet. I heard of children that might have been born if there had been no pet. I heard of children that were bitten by dogs that had given clear signs of serious jealousy but whose owners were unable to part with them.[48]

The owners who said they would die to save their pets might well have been serious. Only four first-class passengers on the RMS *Titanic* died. Anne Isham was one of them: she may have perished because she refused to abandon her Great Dane. Many similarly chose to die alongside their pets in New Orleans when Hurricane Katrina struck in 2005, and when radiation gushed into Fukushima in 2011 Naoto Matsumura stayed to be irradiated and to look after the unevacuated animals.

Pets sometimes help to create and maintain Eden: sometimes they are the snake.

James, Loki's owner, articulated another increasingly common argument for pet ownership:

> It's fairly universally accepted now that the world is massively overpopulated, and humans are having an intensely detrimental effect on the planet.... In order to live in balance with the world around us, our population needs to be limited. People choosing pets over kids is one way of achieving this, without enforcing any draconian measures such as one-child rules, and people are choosing this of their own free will.

Whatever the merits of this argument, it is unlikely, for most, to have anything like the impact of a baby-faced pug, but may, for believers, increase the Eden-like peace generated by their pets. Eden was, after all, a place of ecological bliss and harmony, and if you think that the dog at the hearth is helping to maintain ecological viability, the hearth is likely to be a happier place.

★

Ecology is built on both cooperation and competition, and competition has an important place in pet keeping. Our animals compete vicariously for us, and we give ourselves the credit when, in the park, our dog beats a strange dog in the race for a thrown stick.

That is easy enough to understand. But sometimes the appeal of competition is harder to decode. What can account for the popularity of pedigree dog shows – such as those run by the UK Kennel Club? Success at such shows is judged by the benchmark of compliance with the breed standard. The winner, other things being equal, will be the most typical of the breed. And, for many or most breeds, that means being the most un-doglike – or at least the most un-wolflike. Success demands, too, behaving in the least doglike way: standing 'stacked', for instance, with the feet remaining motionless in the 'correct' position in which the owner has placed them, or 'free stood' – in which the dog adopts and retains the prescribed position itself. Breed champions have no mud on their pristine coats, no deer blood dripping from their lips and no scars from being gored by a wild boar. Their teeth gleam dazzlingly from daily brushing and regular descaling trips to the vet, their breath smells of roses, and a dog with a tendency to flatulence will have had a dose of charcoal that morning to spare the judge's nose. They submit meekly to being prodded by strangers, and know exactly how far from their owners they should run to show off their own legs to the best advantage. A cheap dog, or one which could survive in an Ice Age wood, stands no chance of standing on the podium.

What's going on? It may seem as far from that atavistic camp fire as it's possible to get. But is it? The Supreme Champion is the Supreme Champion not just of the show, but of the genetic race to be maximally cooperative with humans, and so secure its own future and those of its offspring. Cooperation in the Pleistocene might have taken the form of an appetite for human dung; cooperation in the twenty-first-century show ring takes the form of rigid compliance with the breed template and the ability to stand abnormally still. It's tempting to say that natural selection would never smile on the genes of a breed champion, but that would be wrong. The very fact that the champion *is* the champion is a sign of the smile. That dog's genes have an assured future. They may be worth a thousand pounds per ejaculation – which is what a shot of the breed champion's semen might cost.

The run-up to show day and the big day itself both involve very intense cooperation between dog and owner. Show-dog owners talk about their hobby (or business) as a team effort, and they are right. It's not easy for a dog to learn to free-stand, and it is not easy to comb, primp or shampoo a dog, burnish its canines, trim its toenails, learn how to walk so that your rhythm complements the dog's, get up in the early hours to drive it to a distant show, and schmooze the judges – let alone to generate the income necessary to buy a eugenically immaculate dog and get it to the point of stepping sedately into the ring.

This most artificial-looking element of pet ownership, then, is actually one of the most atavistic. As the dog and owner run together in the *V* and the circle before the judges they are – and feel themselves to be – one organism. Crufts is a festival of shamanism: of soul-blending.

I wonder, though, if there is something else behind the tsunami of interest in dog shows. Much of the stress in our lives comes from competition. The shows help to neutralize the power of competition itself – or at least to rehabilitate competition, making it bearable when we return to the office. How? The competition that is the show is seen to be an exercise in the most intimate cooperation. If that is true for a dog show, might it not be true for every instance of competition, if we could only see it properly? If, despite this, competition remains scary, the fact that our dog was trotting beside us through the scariness of the show, as the tame wolf walked beside the child in the Chauvet cave, somehow reduces the trauma of competition per se.

Pedigree shows are not the only shows. Many of the others, if anything, are even more shamanic. You can go straight from classes such as 'best 6 legs', or 'dog most like its owner' to the world depicted on the walls of Pleistocene caves – the world of antler-headed men in the process of transmuting to or from a stag.

★

Modern pet ownership might be atavistic, but pet ownership has changed – and changed in a way that reveals a good deal about us.

I have spent many hours looking at paintings, etchings and prints of men (they're always men) in their homes (usually at the fireside) with the dogs who help them flush, pursue or retrieve game. The man typically leans against the mantelpiece in a tail coat, pulling on a pipe, his face flushed from the exertions of the sporting day. His tired dogs flop on the floor at his feet. The birds, the hares or the deer accounted for during the day are slung on a table, declaring his sovereignty.

The shoot or the hunt in the hinterland is the archetypal leisure activity – followed by far more people over the course of history than have ever just taken a dog for a walk. (Even if you just take the dog for a walk, the dog doesn't see it that way. You might think you're on a peaceful stroll in the park, but the dog is hunting.)

Here is what I think I see in those images. The connection between the man and his dogs is far closer than that between a modern urban pet owner and his dog. The hunting man looks at his dog, and his dog looks at him, with perfect reciprocity, respect and, yes, love.

Distinctions dissolve in these pictures: that between survival skills and enjoyment; between the strenuous and the relaxed; between the wild and the domestic; between working dog and pet; and between the human and the animal. Here, at the fireside, the tail-coated hunter–gatherer atavist is a more normative human than the woman in the Manhattan condo with a diamond-studded cat flap. The boundary between the man and his dog is thin – thinner even than that between the dog-showing owner and the would-be breed champion. The hunter-man and the hunter-dog bleed into one another. It's hard to know where the man ends and the dog begins. That's real pet ownership – ownership of a kind to which the sentimental declarations on the animal tombstones we'll visit in Chapter 8 are dysfunctionally and unsuccessfully groping. The real pet is the wild, killing pet, helping the wild, killing human.

How do pets help us in our leisure? By helping us to be ourselves.

⋆

Our pets can help us to take the hearth out into the world, and to make the world a warmer and less frightening place. (We will look in Chapter 5 at the dog photos on the desks of hard-pressed employees in corporate sweatshops, racing to meet impossible deadlines.) Fish dissolve the toxins of the workplace.

Pets not only warm but enlarge our worlds. Dogs drag us out of our armchairs and out on cardio-protective walks in which we perceive the non-human world with our own sense receptors and recruit our dogs' noses to perceive it more fully. Horses turn their riders into six-legged centaurs and give 6-year-olds the pastoral responsibility and knowledge of an experienced nurse, the perspective of a giant, and the ability to leap a five-barred gate and run at 30 miles an hour. The fish in the tank expose a whole different way of being, as different from ours as the life of an alien in a distant galaxy. They mesmerize, taking us into altered – and usually happier – states of consciousness. Pets infiltrate all areas of our lives and our deaths. We use them as sanitizers, exorcists and sedatives.

Animals soothe us. They may make us healthier in some respects and threaten our health in others. They make us poorer. They make competition – which often bruises us – benign. They may be true friends. They may bond a human family more tightly together, or create a happy, functional human–animal hybrid family. They take us to places we would otherwise avoid. They can create a whole ecosystem – for how else can we describe the cat-centric household, or the community of dog walkers who meet on the local fields?

There is another word for the ecosystem in which we live. We call it 'home'.

The idea of 'home', though, is changing, and the role of pets within it is changing with it *and changing it.*

'Home', for many, is no longer the nuclear family, defined by the presence or hope of children. As we saw when we looked at the effect of pet ownership on the human birth rate, we increasingly prefer animal company to our own. Animals triumph over our most basic biological instinct – the instinct to reproduce. The old order, described in Genesis, of humans at the apex of creation's pyramid, with dominion over non-humans, is being upended. The animals are in charge. *Animal Farm* is real, but the farm is your kitchen.

Simon Garfield observes that a walk through the public rooms and storage areas of the National Gallery in London will yield some two hundred paintings of dogs, most of them seemingly 'incidental'. But he invites us to look again: '[S]o many of the dogs are in charge of the canvas, subtly dominating the image just as they have subtly charmed their creator.'[49]

As for the National Gallery, so for our lives. Pets are redefining 'home'. No longer, often, are pets an added extra – the icing on the familial cake, or a marker of a functional family. Often they *are* the family: *are* the home.

No wonder that our homes – those attempts to recreate Eden – are seen as incomplete without pets. Sometimes, these days, a home won't just be incomplete without a pet; it won't exist at all.

FIVE

The world of work

Work, for most of our history as a species, has been primarily the collection – from bushes and the bodies of animals – of the calories we need to survive. That is still the most important function of work. We go to the office so that we can hunt, gather and forage in the supermarket. Companion animals played and still sometimes play an important part in calorie collection. They run down deer, leap into icy ponds to collect downed ducks, see off predators, and gather sheep from the hill. Cats kill the mice and rats which rob the granaries.

The UK is a nation of animal – and particularly dog – lovers. But what do we think dogs should *really* be doing? What are they *for*? Don't dog lovers, at some level, know that their inner-city pets aren't living their best life? Does anyone really think that bows, tartan coats, elaborate coiffure and organic pheasant terrine in the food bowl do their dog justice? Aren't all the treats an attempt to assuage the guilt that comes from forcing the dog to be something other than itself? We know that proper dogs work. What other explanation can there be for the colossal success of the long-running series *One Man and His Dog*, which began in 1976 as part of BBC1's *Countryfile*, is still going, and in the early 1980s had audiences of over 8 million?[1]

Amongst that 8 million must have been many owners of panting brachycephalics. How could they not curl their toes in shame when they watched the border collies – so plainly in touch with their lupine past – dashing, prowling, loping and slinking?

But are we comparing like with like? Are those lithe, smart sheepdogs something completely different from sedentary pet dogs? Is a pet by definition an animal that doesn't work, or isn't economically useful?

★

'Is Maisie a pet?', I asked Greg, a farmer in North Devon, of his sheepdog. 'Course she's not', replied Greg. 'She's a worker.'

But Maisie and Greg are inseparable. She pads with him through the Barnstaple shops, plays cricket with him on the beach, watches hopefully as he fishes for bass, and curls up next to him when he's dozing in front of the TV.

Maisie is a pet if ever there was one. It's just that she's doing what pets were originally ordained by evolution to do. She's the real thing. If it doesn't seem that way, it is because Greg doesn't build divisions across his life. There's no nine-til-five-ness. He's just alive, with his dog at his side. He's farming when he shops, fishes, plays cricket and watches the television, and Maisie, all the time, is hunting or dreaming about hunting or sleeping so that she can hunt more vigorously when she wakes up.

Greg is an old-fashioned farmer. His cows aren't just the numbers on their ear tags. They have names: Molly, Samantha and Jodie. He pulled them himself out of their mothers, slaps them affectionately on the back, knows all their peccadillos, keeps a careful eye on their health and, though he's usually an unsentimental man, has been known to shed a tear when he loads them into the trailer to go off to the abattoir. He can't bear to go with them. His son drives the Land Rover instead.

Are Molly, Samantha and Jodie pets? Of course not, says Greg; and this time I believe him. The difference isn't because Greg is instrumental in the cows' deaths. He'll take his shotgun to Maisie when she's in pain and he can't do anything more for her. Rather it is because the cows exist to die, whereas Maisie exists to live, just as Greg himself does. Greg and Maisie share the project of being alive, which is a robust kind of solidarity, and they help one another with that project in ways that the cows can't – or at least don't. Greg will eventually die, but it'll be a Maisie kind of dying, not a Molly kind of dying.

Few of us today look much like Upper Palaeolithic hunter–gatherers with our dogs at our sides to sniff out wild boar for spearing, or like Neolithic farmers controlling our cattle-herding dogs with an arcane vocabulary of whistles. Most of us leave the dog, the cat and the budgie at home, or, at punishing rates, with some sort of carer (the animal charity Blue Cross states that doggy day care typically costs between £20 and £45 per day, though it can be a good deal more).[2]

If we can, though, many of us choose to have our pets around us as we work – just as Greg has Maisie with him. It suggests that we see our pets as part of us, or at least as facilitators of our thriving at work: as co-workers. We have already visited the dog-filled Amazon offices in Seattle. Amazon, the supreme masters at squeezing productivity out of their people, know that people, even if they are not sheep-herders, do their jobs better with dogs.

It suggests too that we see our *real* work as work for which we need animals. Even if we're in an office on the top floor of a Canary Wharf skyscraper we're still, really, trying to kill that boar for supper.

Even in the West it is only lately that most of us have given up all personal farming and delegated our farming and our animal-killing to others. In the tiny yards behind suffocating inner city tenements there was, until recently, a pig waiting to be stuck and brined, or a few strutting fowl. Go to modern-day Cairo and you will see pigeon lofts rising high above the apartment blocks. A Cairene may spend his day driving a taxi or filling in a ledger, but he is still a farmer who sees his stock as pets (witness his delight at seeing his birds wheel back to the loft from the desert, and his tender and wholly unnecessary stroking of the birds at the nest).

We hang on to our prehistoric pasts as best we can. We try to be Upper Palaeolithic when we go camping, hiking, fishing and shooting (even if we only shoot tin cans with an air rifle at the showground), and if we can't bring ourselves to kill we hunt birds with binoculars. In our Neolithic moments we tend gardens, allotments and window boxes, grow cress on wet cotton wool, volunteer to work at the city farm, and, of course, we sit down with our microwaved meal to watch working sheepdogs on a screen. And since prehistoric people had day jobs with animals, we do too if and in so far as we can. We work best in the context we've evolved for. And that means animals at our desk.

It's a fair bet that animals were there at the birth of desk jobs, as they are there at the birth of gods and saints. We have no depictions of the scribes in the early Mesopotamian states who kept accounts and compiled king lists in early cuneiform. But dogs were there too, and surely they helped to convince the scribes, in the radically new world of the bureaucrat, that their new way of being was still a way of *human* being.

Animals have been at the writer's side ever since. St Jerome is famously pictured slaving at his translation of the Vulgate in the company of a dog and a lion. Dogs and cats are common in mediaeval depictions of scholars at work (the animal is typically curled up, asleep, on the scholar's desk), and it has been suggested that this is because dogs symbolize the good scholar's fidelity to the truth, nose for falsehood, and relentless pursuit of a goal. Dogs, too, sadly but more realistically, are associated with the planet Saturn, which brings the melancholy which often characterizes academic life.[3] No doubt there is some truth in this, but no doubt, too, these associations were a result of scholars having dogs in their study to keep them company. Nobody ever bought a dog because it symbolized either Saturn or dogged intellectual inquiry.

Cats were important comforters for bored and lonely monks, stooping over their lecterns. One young monk in a Benedictine monastery in Austria extolled his companion in a poem scribbled in Old Irish in the margin of a copy of St Paul's epistles, about the close of the eighth century.

I and Pangur Ban, my cat,
'Tis a like task we are at;
Hunting mice is his delight,
Hunting words I sit all night.
Better far than praise of men
'Tis to sit with book and pen;
Pangur bears me no ill-will,
He, too, plies his simple skill.
'Tis a merry thing to see
At our tasks how glad are we,
When at home we sit and find
Entertainment to our mind.
Oftentimes a mouse will stray
In the hero Pangur's way;
Oftentimes my keen thought set
Takes a meaning in its net.
'Gainst the wall he sets his eye
Full and fierce and sharp and sly;
'Gainst the wall of knowledge I
All my little wisdom try.
When a mouse darts from its den,
O! how glad is Pangur then;
O! what gladness do I prove

When I solve the doubts I love.
So in peace our task we ply,
Pangur Ban, my cat, and I;
In our arts we find our bliss,
I have mine, and he has his.
Practice every day has made
Pangur perfect in his trade;
I get wisdom day and night,
Turning darkness into light.[4]

The cat and the monk are about the same business. They are both hunters.

Monasteries and nunneries were places of hard work: of copying, scholarship, agriculture, brewing, worship and prayer. While the implicit commission of the home was to model Eden, the explicit commission of monastic houses was to bring about Eden by disciplined graft. Not only were animals a crucial part of Eden; they were valued co-grafters. In mediaeval books of hours, pets of various kinds (but usually cats and dogs) are often close to praying people, as if they are joining in with the prayers, helping to translate them into a different language.

So common was mediaeval monastic pet-keeping that the authorities (while generally turning a blind eye to the pets themselves) sometimes felt that they had to lay down some rules. Bishop William of Wykeham, in 1387, issued an edict to nunneries under his jurisdiction, declaring that pets must not be taken into church,[5] though it was sometimes recognized that pets might fill a gap that God could not fill: a monk from Canterbury wrote to Lady Honor Liske, in 1536: 'I have sent unto you … a beast, the creature of God, sometime wild, but now tame, to comfort your heart at such time as you be weary of praying.'[6]

It may have been concern about the effect of animals on the spiritual lives of college inmates that caused the fourteenth-century statutes of All Souls College and New College, Oxford, to outlaw any kind of dog and, in a fifteenth-century revision, ferrets too.[7]

Efforts such as those at All Souls and New College failed to break the age-old synergy of animal and writer. Examples litter literary history. Walter Scott told a friend that he found writing almost impossible unless a dog was at his feet; his wolfhound, Nym, always escorted him from his desk to the bookshelves and a portrait of his cat, Hinse, was on his writing desk. Dogs prowl through his pages. As Darwin wrote *The Expressions of the Emotions in Man and Animals* (1872), Polly, his terrier, snored in a basket by his feet. Virginia Woolf's sheepdog, Garth, went with her to the London Library.

Pets are not only theological and literary assistants: they oil the wheels of commerce, and are commonly depicted in shops and professional spaces, sometimes looking interestedly on at the business in hand, but more often sleeping or playing, normalizing the workplace and making it seem like an extension of home.

★

Pets at work are not always a good thing. A fifteenth-century monk in Deventer in the Netherlands unwisely left his manuscript open on his desk overnight. The next day there was an almost blank page, with just this written on it:

> Here is nothing missing, but a cat peed on this page during the night. Cursed be the pest of a cat that peed on this book during the night in Deventer and because of it, many others too. And beware not to leave books open at night where cats can get at them.[8]

John Steinbeck would have sympathized. His Mexican setter puppy 'made confetti of about half of my manuscript book [*Of Mice and Men*]', he lamented to his agent, in the original 'the dog ate my homework' letter. 'There was no other draft. I was pretty mad but the poor little fellow may have been acting critically.'[9] And animals, often a calming influence, are not always so. Dickens, sitting in Tavistock Square in 1852, trying to finish *Bleak House*, was 'driven Mad by Dogs' barking outside his window.[10]

Most of us cannot take our pets literally to work with us, or work in a place where they are. But such is our pets' importance to our well-being and sense of identity that we find ways of having them – or some other congenial animal – beside us. We might have a nodding dog stuck to the car windscreen as we drive to work. When we get to the office we may have a photo of a laughing dog on the desk, next to the photos of the laughing children. Often the child is photographed holding the dog: who, then, is the real subject of adoration? Or perhaps we don't distinguish between them: perhaps they are one entity – a totem of home and refuge? The hair of a beloved dead cat might be embedded in a bracelet around our wrist, guiding from beyond the grave our right hand as it does the work of the day; or the nail clippings from a much-mourned dog might rest in a pendant over our heart, governing the passion we bring to our annual appraisal.

Even if we are coy about such personal mementos, do we not surreptitiously watch dogs doing tricks on YouTube or Instagram in the lunch hour, or kittens just being kittens, adorably, when we should be writing that crucial report? Why, if we don't need to be reminded constantly of our defining alliances with animals, did our ancestors carry walking sticks fashioned like dogs' heads, and wear ties emblazoned with horses' hoofs?

⋆

Not only do pets help (and sometimes hinder) us in in our work; they are hugely important in marketing.

In 1972, Andrex, the toilet paper company, had 23 per cent of the market share. Then the famous puppy scampered across our screens and billboards, carrying toilet paper and the company's destiny with it. Andrex now has nearly twice the market share of its nearest competitor.[11]

Andrex was not the first to realize the pulling power of animals. In the 1880s Frederick Morgan's painting 'The Bath: His Turn Next' was used to devastating effect to sell Pears soap. A young girl hands a small dog to her little brother, sitting in the bathtub. A 2008 study found that nearly 18 per cent of internet advertisements contained animal images;[12] a 2001 study that nearly a quarter of Super Bowl advertisements featured animals.[13] Pet species (and particularly dogs and cats) were used more than other species.[14] Keller and Gierl, (2020) asked why pet images were so compelling, and concluded that the use of pets resulted in 'more favorable brand attitudes, feelings of entertainment, and message credibility compared to the images of human characters and undomesticated animal characters. With respect to animal trustworthiness, the pets are perceived as superior to undomesticated animals'.[15]

We have seen this motif before. An alliance with animals makes humans seem safer and more desirable. Pets lend humans moral status. 'Cuteness' itself can help, the study found, but the use of 'cute' baby animals makes potential buyers worry about exploitation, cancelling out the benefit. Cuteness in adult animals, though, is very powerful. It ignites our nurturing instincts, and the innocence of baby-faced animals makes us feel that the product itself must be trustworthy and its sellers incapable of deceit. Keller and Gierl trace the appeal of animals back into prehistory, linking the ability of puppies to sell toilet paper to the impulse that led our forebears to carve the Lion Man of Hohlenstein-Stadel (35,000–41,000 years ago) and paint the walls of the Lascaux caves (*c.* 17,000 years ago).

The archetypal advert using a pet is the Jack Russell-type terrier, Nipper, in Francis Barraud's 1890s painting, listening intently to 'His Master's Voice' coming through the horn of the gramophone. The image speaks of an intimate, almost clairvoyant connection between the human and the non-human world – a connection thought to be desirable. Just look at the HMV sales figures.

Whether we are working or buying, animals generate comfort. That comfort comes by generating a sense of normativity. Humans are themselves, and can thrive properly, when they are in the company of animals, and endorsed by those animals. Humans by themselves aren't what they are meant to be; aren't what they might be.

★

Not only can pets generate big business; they *are* big business. We have seen already the financial scale of the pet industry and its associated economies. Where there are huge profits to be made there are always huge numbers of shady operators. In the pet industry, puppy farms – sometimes known as puppy mills – are common. Whelping bitches are typically kept in small pens, isolated from one another, and bear several litters each year. Because a rapid turnover of puppies maximizes profits, the puppies are taken from their mothers too young, inadequately socialized, and their health is often permanently compromised.

A little easy research usually makes it obvious when an animal has come from a puppy farm; but if you don't look, you don't see. A survey of UK pet owners for the PDSA showed that nearly a quarter of owners conducted no research at all before buying a pet.[16] This suggests a kind of wilful, Nelsonian blindness – the same sort of blindness necessary to avoid noting the wretchedness of a brachycephalic animal.

Pet owners generally mean well. Brachycephalic animals are sincerely cherished. They and other animals are bought for companionship, home completion, self-completion and for the other reasons discussed in this book. That they are often bought blindly, and remain, though the apple of their owners' eyes, in a total blind spot is curious and significant. Pets have become instrumentalized: fashioned into useful horrors by the industry and by the neuroses they palliate in their owners.

This instrumentalization is abetted by another great pet-related industry: veterinary medicine. James Herriot is long gone. Tweedy Tristan Farnon would share no common language with the modern, sleek, superspecialist in surgical scrubs. The industry is now dominated by vast, aggressive corporates, coupled in infernal synergy with pet insurance companies. There is concern that the profit motive of the big corporates results in overinvestigation and overtreatment; that animal welfare is a casualty. Morale in the veterinary profession is another casualty.[17] Veterinary education doesn't help. 'Soft' relational skills are under-taught. The job of a veterinary surgeon is too often seen as the diagnosis and treatment of a problem, rather than the care of a whole animal and the context in which it lives. A cat may have kidney disease, but the cat is more than its kidneys, and the relationship between the owner and the cat is *much* more than the kidneys. James Herriot never treated a disordered metabolic pathway, a gene, a syndrome, a prolapse or an economic unit: he treated both the animal and the owner from whom the animal was inseparable. That's hard to do if the accountants of the big veterinary corporate are breathing down your neck.

Veterinary medicine can make animals disappear – and not just with a syringe full of deadly barbiturates. It can magic them away, substituting clinical conundrums or spreadsheet entries in the place where Rover once was.

SIX

Society, politics and war

The Ojibwe people are part of the Anishinaabe clan system of the Great Lakes and northern plains of America. Their language contains the word *doodem*, which, bastardized, becomes *totem*. It has come to refer to a belief system which asserts that each clan, and perhaps each individual in a clan, has a non-human guide or guides (rather akin to angels in the Christian tradition). The guide is typically an animal, which both reflects and affects the attributes of its charge. You do not choose your totem animal: it chooses you. The Ojibwe themselves consider that each individual has nine animal guides, and representations, misrepresentations and baroque perversions of the Ojibwe beliefs can be found on the shelves of any New Age bookshop and on countless websites. One typical website declares that a cat represents and curates: 'Guardianship, detachment, sensuality, mystery, magic, independence', and being 'astute and watchful'.[1] But cats did not reach America until the early seventeenth century, by which time the Anishinaabe tradition of spirit animals was already ancient.

Spirit animals are known to many cultures (we will meet the 'familiars' of European witches in Chapter 7), and there is a long and complex debate about how much one can generalize about their function and the metaphysical schemes into which they fit.

The debate does not matter for our purposes. One generalization is uncontroversial: individuals and groupings of individuals have commonly felt that an animal represents their character, and sometimes their interests. The animal may be more or less important: it may guide or intercede; it may simply embody an actual or desirable character.

A typical New Age account of shamanic teaching about spirit animals declares that 'every child born has an ethereal being (a guardian angel) in the form of an animal'. This 'protective spirit', the totem animal, stays with us all our life, accompanying us 'throughout our spiritual development, alerting [us] when danger is imminent, and indicating when a change in life is expected'. We, ideally, should cooperate with the spirit.

> When we pay attention to the nature totem and pay tribute to it, we are actually bowing our heads in front of the forces behind it, we connect with these forces and with their help, we can have a clearer understanding of our own living conditions. We can share in their power, their 'magic power'.

In nature totems, man objectifies the energies that permeate his life in a symbolic form.[2]

This will sound wildly eccentric to many – many who are unembarrassed by the lion and the unicorn on the United Kingdom's royal coat of arms, or the red dragon on the Welsh flag.

What do our national animals, official and unofficial, say about us? What can we conclude about the Faroe Islands from their adoption of the oystercatcher as their national bird? The United Kingdom has no *official* national animal at all. What does that mean? Are nations without a national animal confident – rightly or wrongly – that they don't need a model for nationhood, or any help in achieving it? Some nations recruit many official national animals, from all quarters of the animal kingdom. Finland, for instance, has the brown bear, the whooper swan, the perch, the Holly Blue butterfly and the seven-spot ladybird; and Pakistan the Indus river dolphin, the markhor (a huge goat), the red-legged partridge, the snow leopard, the shaheen falcon and the Indus crocodile. Greece, though it could choose from many actual birds, has selected the mythical phoenix. Palestine has enlisted the Arabian mountain gazelle and the Palestine sunbird (the orange-tufted sunbird) in its project of nation-building, and Moldova's national animal is the aurochs, which has been extinct for a long time, but which is the parent of modern cattle.

One can weave many theses around each of these choices – many spurious, some perhaps suggestive. My point here is not what each animal in fact says, but that they are thought to say *something*: that they declare an assumed and important connection between people and the non-human world.

There are no true pet species amongst the official animals of the nations (though a case might be made for the Karabakh horse of Azerbaijan, the Canadian horse of Canada, the cow of Nepal, the camel of Saudi Arabia, the Asian elephant and the Siamese fighting fish of Thailand). Sometimes, but rarely, pet animals officially represent parts of a country (such as the Akita dog for the Akita prefecture of Japan and the Chihuahua for the Mexican state of Chihuahua). But the general pattern is clear: when a nation wants a guardian angel, it chooses a wild thing. That, I suggest, is not because pet animals are not considered sufficiently qualified for the job, but because they are already doing it. They do not need to be enrolled.

There are *unofficial* pet totems of various nations. The obvious example is the British bulldog (PLATE 21). But generally they have not sunk deep into the national psyche: they tend simply to provide a convenient shorthand for describing national characteristics that are already generally recognized – or at least asserted.

1. Statuette of Bastet, the Egyptian cat goddess, 664–630 BCE. Where do pets end and gods begin?

2. Loved in life and honoured in death. A Roman grave stele depicting a dog, 150–200 CE.

3. 'Beware of the dog' (*Cave canem*) in a Roman mosaic, c.100 CE.

4. The North African King Garamantes, taken captive by his enemies, is rescued by a pack of his loyal dogs. Illumination from a bestiary, 1201–25.

ternio nature .ē. extra hominem esse non posse; Item.

Legitur
tum suos
duos. ũ.g
tē regē ab
eis captũa
dia man
tũ. ducen
nes agm
to. p medi
eis inimico
ab exilio r
runt p liam
ũsus resist
Jasone lic
fecto cani
aspnat̃ cu
edia obiũ
machi re

flāme se iniecit. accenso rogo dñi sui. ꝛ pariť igni absumptus .ē.
pio nunnopictimo cõsulib; dãpnatũ dñm canis cũ ambigi ñ
poss; comitat̃ in carcerem. mox pcussũ ululatu psecut̃ .ē.
sumq; ex miseratione ppli romani potestas ei fieret cibi. ad
os defuncti escã tulit; Vltimo inde deiectũ in tyberim cadav
adnatans sustentare conat̃; Iam ũũ uestigiũ lepors cũ nere
perit. atq; ad durticelin seruit uenit. ꝛ qddã marũ cõpitũ. qd pa
tes in plurimas scindit. obiciens singlarũ semitar̃ exordia tacit

5. As a species, humans grew up with animals. We made domesticated animals what they are. Adam names the animals: illumination from a medieval bestiary, 1201–25.

6. Kindness reciprocated? Saintliness recognized? St Roch is offered bread by his dog: illumination from a French prayer book, 1500.

7. Pets are commonly seen in depictions of pivotal moments in religious history. Van Eyck, *The Birth of John the Baptist*, from the Turin-Milan Book of Hours, 1422.

8. Medieval cats make themselves busy: illumination from a medieval bestiary, 1226–50.

Musio appellatus quod muribus infestus
sit. Hunc uulgus catum a captura
uocant. Alii dicunt quod captat id est
uidet. Nam tam acute cernit ut fulgore lumi
nis noctis tenebras superet. Unde a greco uenit
catus id est ingeniosus. apotoykagestai.

Mus pusillum
animal grecum
illi nomen est
quicquid uero ex eo trahitur
latinum fit. Alii dicunt
mures quod ex humore terre nascantur. Nam
mus terra. unde et humus. Huius in plenilunio
iecur crescit. sicut quedam maritima augentur.
que rursus minuente luna deficiunt. Sorex

9. Unusual pets have long been a mark of a Bohemian personality. Giovanni Bazzi (Il Sodoma): self-portrait with his pet badgers, 1502.

10. A cat, an icon of domestic harmony, rests at the feet of Adam and Eve before the Fall shatters the harmony. Dürer, 1504.

11. Human and dog together worship the newborn Christ: fragment from a tapestry cartoon, after Raphael, 1518.

12. Though more or less destitute, in a crumbling house, Sorgheloos is content because his dog and cat companionably share his poverty. Painted glass roundel, Dutch, 1510–20.

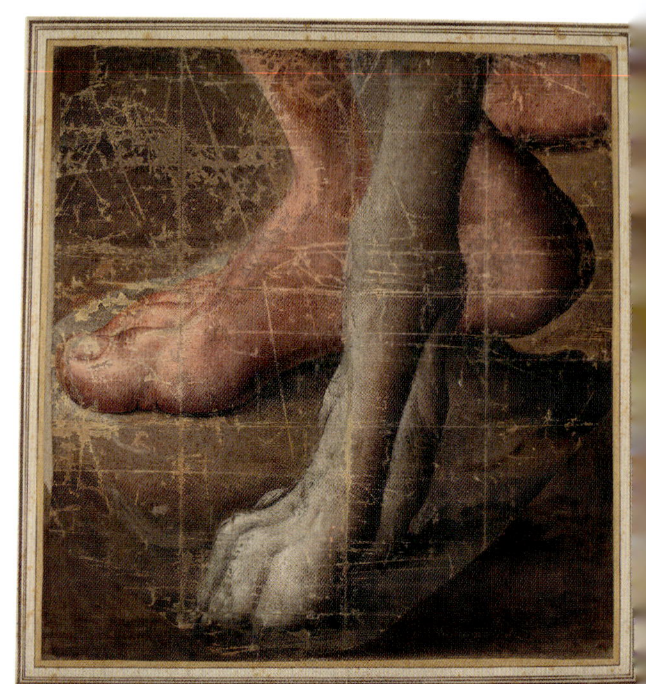

13. A dog and a cat as two sides of a human personality. Portrait by Dosso Dossi, 1508–10.

14. A long way from wolves: Tudor dogs, 1520–30.

15. Dogs around a kebab seller in Constantinople, from a late-sixteenth-century picture book of the Ottoman Empire.

Hic Coquus quidam est, qui Iecur, & eiusmodi uiscerum par
tes apparari studet, quibus saginant Canes, plateis quotidie
in plurimos utrobique sepultos, quem passim modico aere ciuib:
plateis inhabitantibus diuendit.

16. An eighteenth-century dog fetches a stick: Stukeley notebook, 1705.

17. The silk-lined velvet-covered kennel made for Marie Antoinette's dog, *c.*1775–80.

18. Majnun, the hero of an Arab epic, is surrounded by animals, attracted by the purity of his love for Layla, his childhood sweetheart, in this Mughal version, c.1700.

19. Poise meets poise: A Qajar lady with her cat. Shiraz, Iran, 1811.

豊国画

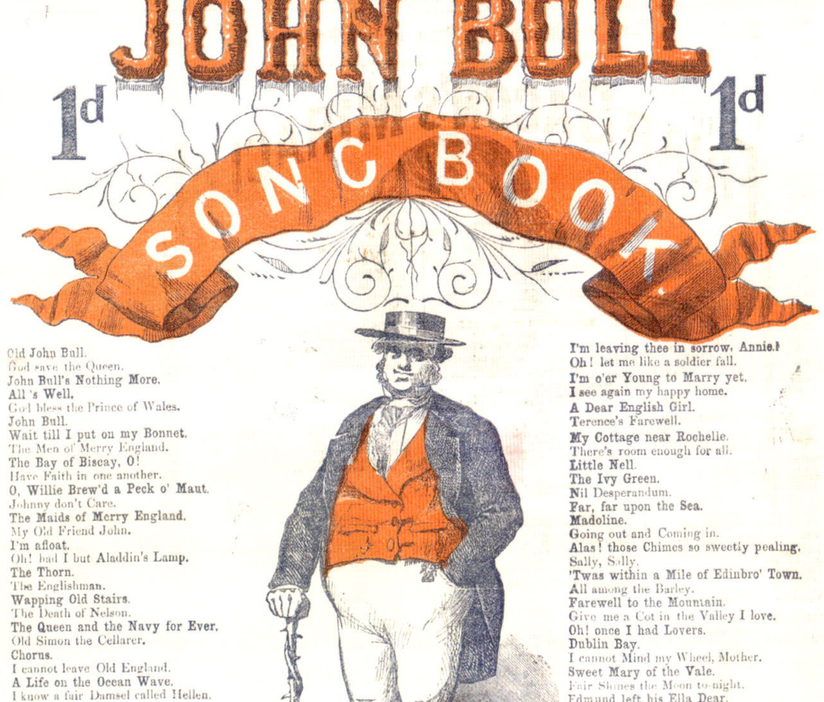

20. Pets as fashion accessories: a Pekinese dog sits on its owner's shoulder. Japan, c.1801.

21. Animals as national icons: a bulldog, with a face very like his master, stands beside John Bull, the quintessential Englishman, c.1850.

SPRATT'S PATENT LIMITED
SPECIALLY PREPARED
LARK
FOOD
ALSO FOR
THRUSHES, BLACKBIRDS,
& INSECTIVIROUS
BIRDS.

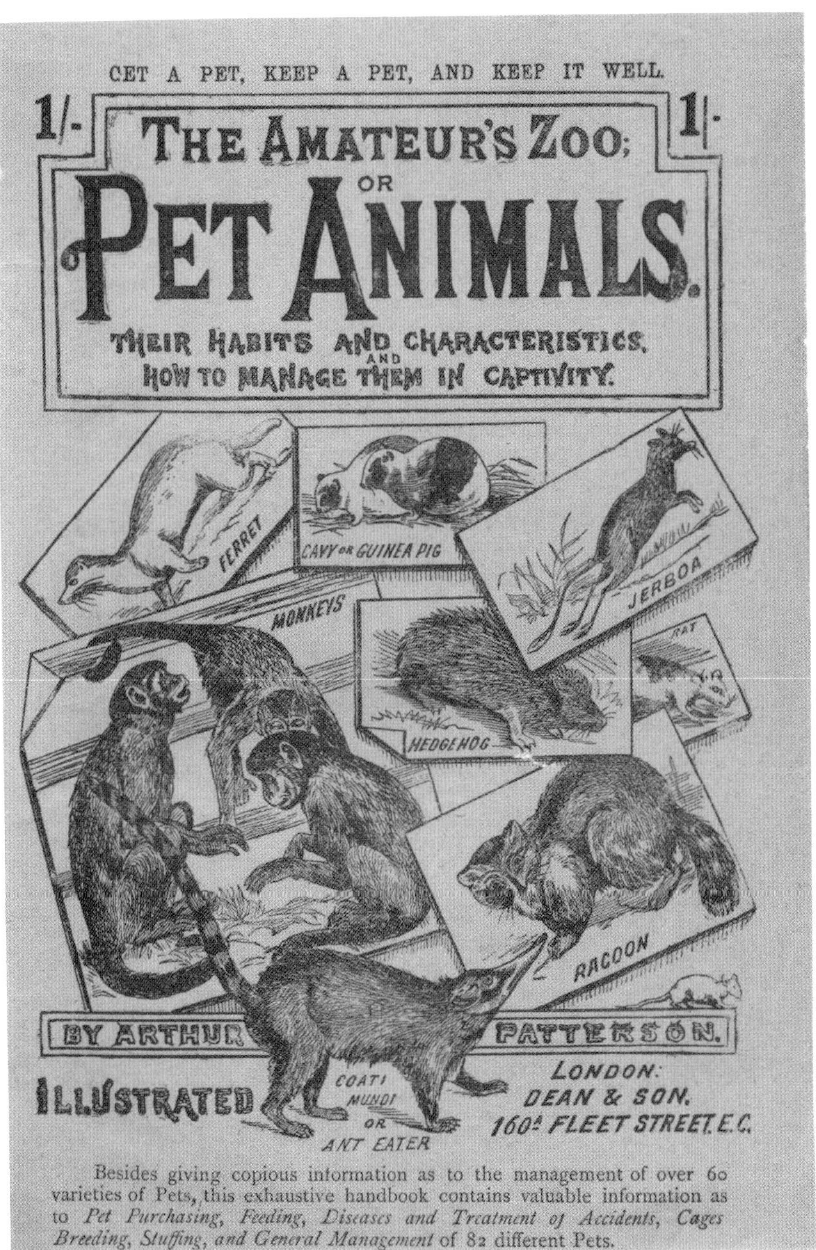

22. Bringing the heavens into the home: advertisement for Spratt's bird food, 1885–95.

23. Not just dogs and cats: how to turn the home into a zoo, 1889.

24. Putting a ribbon round a cat's neck doesn't de-wild it: it remains a predator. Illustration c.1880.

26. 'Can't you talk?', G.A. Holmes's painting, used in advertisements, c.1890s. But is the child or the dog asking the question?

26. Caring owners, says this advertisement (*c.*1890), bath their dogs just as they bath their children.

27. Humanizing cats, or cat-izing humans? Louis Wain, *Days in Catland, Father Tuck's Panorama*, 1901.

28. Whym Chow, the dog beloved by 'Michael Field', and celebrated posthumously in a collection of passionate and very theological poems, 1896.

29. Pets often look like their owners. But who selects, or changes, whom? Physician Sir Henry Acland with his pet monkey, photographed by his daughter, Sarah Angelina Acland, 1896.

30. The fox-cub mascot of no. 32 Squadron, Humières aerodrome, France, May 1918.

31. A fox and a rabbit reflect different elements of a human personality. Postcard, 1958, echoing Dossi (PLATE 13).

32. Pets as guarantors of political integrity: the Franklin D. Roosevelt memorial, Washington DC, featuring Roosevelt's Scottish terrier Fala, dedicated 1997.

THEY (WHO) SEEK TO ESTABLISH
SYSTEMS OF GOVERNMENT BASED ON
THE REGIMENTATION OF ALL HUMAN
BEINGS BY A HANDFUL OF INDIVIDUAL
RULERS... CALL THIS A NEW ORDER.
IT IS NOT NEW AND IT IS NOT ORDER.

FAST AND LOW.

Dealer. "I CAN HIGHLY RECOMMEND THIS NEW BREED, MADAME! MOST UP-TO-DATE AND FASHIONABLE DOG IN THE MARKET."

33. 'I can highly recommend this new breed, Madame! Most up-to-date and fashionable dog in the market.' Designer dogs in a *Punch* cartoon by George Morrow, 1910.

34. Dogs as quasi-persons: public transport tickets for dogs, c.1950s.

35. Powders for pets to 'prevent any tendency towards hysteria during an air raid': 1940s.

36. Where do dogs end and their humans begin? An English child following in the furry footsteps of his shamanic forebears: ?1930s.

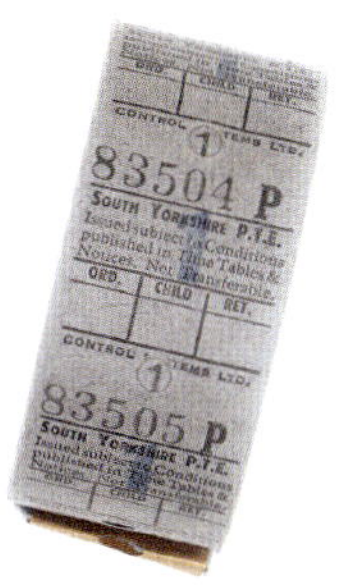

AIR RAID POWDERS

A.R.P.

For Puppies, Dogs and Cats.

These Powders will NOT harm your pet.

This powder dulls the nervous system immediately and prevents any tendency towards hysteria during an air raid. Another dose may be given four hours later if necessary.

As soon as the first warning is heard, give the powder on the tongue or in a little milk.

DOSE—Half powder for puppy, one powder for medium dog, two powders for large dog, one for cat.

SHAW'S VETERINARY PRODUCTS, LTD.
Canine House, 1325 London Road, Norbury, S.W.16.

This packet contains two powders for 6d.

37. Members of the congregation at the entrance to the dog chapel, Vermont, USA.

38. Pet burial, Rossendale Pet Cemetery, Lancashire, c.1980.

39. Tombstone for Rex, Rossendale Pet Cemetery.

"REX"
14 YEARS
OF PLEASURE AND FUN
ENDED BY
A HIT AND RUN.

40. Pets as social adhesive: Walter the college cat at Exeter College, Oxford, 2024.

At the birth of ancient nations, states and cities, however, it may have been different. Laura Hobgood-Oster makes the intriguing suggestion that the foundation myth of Rome might have adopted and assimilated the conversion of wolves to dogs to symbolize Rome's emergence from the dark anarchy of the wild. Tradition, she writes, calls the suckler of Romulus and Remus a 'she-wolf', but

> the earliest depiction, the Capitoline Wolf, which is reproduced endlessly, is decidedly dog-like, with a shorter nose and more defined forehead. The two boys hang on her; and, through her adoption and care of them, she literally guarantees that Rome (and later its Empire) will emerge. Such stories of the founding of human culture are naturally intertwined with canines.[3]

Many organizations – including universities, schools, sports teams and so on – have animal mascots, but they too, like the unofficial animals of the nations, rarely signify much. They are mere badges. Any other distinctive badge would do just as well. The identity and coherence of such smaller entities needs no bolstering – or, if it does, is not meaningfully bolstered by a ceremonial wombat on the crest. Yet real live animals do matter to institutions. I have mentioned already Walter, the cat at my own Oxford college, who has his own honoured and inviolable home just outside the Porters' Lodge, and has become a symbol of the *homeliness* of the place. It's that recurrent theme: pet animals create home wherever they are. Perhaps, when official national animals really mean something, that is what they are doing: making a nation feel like home to its inhabitants.

There is a curious related phenomenon. Classroom pets are the national animals of the class. There is intense competition amongst children to take the classroom pet home for the holidays. Why should there be such an unseemly scrabble for the privilege? It is hardly explained by mere affection for the animal, which will have been systematically ignored during term time by the children who now clamour for custody. Rather, I suspect, it is an attempt to normalize school: to make the classroom cosily continuous with home. It is another example of animals as mediators between different domains. They did it in prehistory, brokering commerce between the quotidian world and the spirit world – a task that totemic spirit animals still undertake for believers. They drain toxins from the workplace, and from competition itself. They make peace between people and their own psyches, calming them, and make strangers talk to one another.

Animals may sometimes be crude tools of a state, an institution or a ruler. Elephants, tamed but not domesticated, declared the power of many an eastern potentate. If (the message is) I can get an animal this big and this dangerous to walk in a straight line, bedecked with garlands, and with my queen swaying in a box on its back, are there any limits to my sovereignty? What might I not do to you?

There are many military mascots, and for obvious reasons pet species feature prominently. A badger or moose would not behave on a parade ground.

A few examples. Amongst the first recorded instances of military mascots (there must have been many earlier mascots) are the vultures caught by Marius' army in the second century BCE during Marius' campaign against the Germanic tribes. They were fitted with bronze collars and released, and the flashing bronze was taken as a sign that they would soon glut on the corpses of Rome's enemies.[4] In the American Civil War the 8th Wisconsin Regiment was accompanied by a bald eagle – 'Old Abe the War Eagle' – who was wounded twice. Sallie Ann Jarrett, a bull terrier who belonged to (no, was one of) the Pennsylvania Volunteers and guarded their dead and wounded, was killed in action in 1865 and has her own memorial statue in Gettysburg National Military Park.

Formal British regimental mascots (regarded as members of the regiment, often holding a rank and maintained with public money) really date from 1775, when a wild goat wandered onto the Bunker Hill battlefield and escorted the colour party of the embattled Royal Welsh Fusiliers to safety. The regiment and its successors have marched after a goat ever since, and given the goat of the day Guinness to drink and two cigarettes a day to eat.

The Royal Welsh goats have not always covered themselves in glory. In 2006, when leading a parade before the queen, Lance Corporal William ('Bill') Windsor (the goat) got overexcited, broke rank and tried to butt the drummers. He was demoted to fusilier, and no longer had to be saluted. He was eventually rehabilitated, his rank restored, and was retired honourably to Whipsnade Zoo.

Such stories are fun, but I doubt – as I doubt the significance of other mascots – that these relationships add much to the cohesion or identity of a regiment. They generate personal loyalties, no doubt, but that is different.

The personal loyalties are not always unilateral: they are sometimes felt acutely by the animal. Boxer, a Staffordshire Bull Terrier which was a mascot of the Staffordshire Regiment, was accidentally left behind in Cairo in 1882 when the troop train went without him. He followed the tracks for about 240 miles, finally being reunited with the soldiers in Assiut.

Boxer's story recalls the tale of Xanthippus' dog, told by Plutarch. In 480 BCE Greek sailors set out from Piraeus to engage the Persians at Salamis, leaving their frantic relatives weeping on the quayside. Xanthippus' dog, unable to bear being parted from his master, leapt into the sea and swam 10 miles alongside the trireme to Salamis, where he tottered ashore and fell dead from exhaustion.

True pets, unsurprisingly, give true solace to soldiers far from home and facing terrible danger. The First World War trenches, and many other theatres of war, were home to animals which were there simply to give comfort: dogs, birds, cats and small mammals. As pets do everywhere, they generated an aura of home, and soothed raw nerves. Many an orphaned dog was adopted, and found to be an adopter itself. Wherever an animal was allowed to be truly itself – truly animal – it *humanized* the humans it met. Emmanuel Levinas tells of 'Bobby', a dog who happened to find his way into a Nazi POW camp. Bobby, said Levinas, came to the prisoners' morning parade and waited for them when they returned from their hard labour, 'jumping up and down and barking in delight'. The Nazis saw the Jewish prisoners as non-human. But Bobby had 'no doubt that we were human', and convinced doubting prisoners that they were.[5]

As we have seen already when looking at farmers' dogs, merely having a use other than being a pet does not stop an animal being a true pet. Michael Morpurgo's *War Horse* (1982)[6] and Steven Spielberg's 2011 film adaptation of the book dramatically illustrate the relationships between Joey, a horse deployed by the British Army in the Great War, and various people amongst whom he is thrown by the tides of war. War dogs – employed to sniff out mines or improvised explosive devices, perform sentry duty,[7] carry messages or medical supplies and hunt for casualties and enemies – were as loved and valued as the most mission-free pet, and loved and valued their human friends too. Wojtek, an 18-stone Syrian-born brown bear who became the mascot of a Polish artillery supply company in the Second World War, and carried big shells and boxes of ammunition in the battle of Monte Cassino, was devoted to his soldier friends, and wrestled affectionately with them.

Sometimes the devotion is even more dramatic. Take, for instance, Rifleman Kahn, a German Shepherd dog attached to the Cameronians in the Second World War. He was with his handler, Lance

Corporal Jimmy Muldoon, when their assault craft came under fire and capsized, throwing Jimmy – who couldn't swim – into the water. Kahn grabbed Jimmy's jacket in his teeth and dragged him to shore. After the war, Jimmy asked Kahn's owners, who had lent the dog to the army, if he could keep him. At first they refused, but, when they saw how strong the bond between the man and the dog was, they relented, and Jimmy and Kahn stayed together for the rest of Kahn's life.[8]

There are many other wartime examples of animal loyalty. Take Judy, an English pointer held with British sailors imprisoned by the Japanese in the Second World War, who crept out of the camp to find food for the starving prisoners and barked to distract the guards when they were beating the POWs; or Jet, an Alsatian trained as a rescue dog, who with his handler Corporal Wardle recovered 150 people from buildings destroyed in the Blitz. On one occasion, having located a woman trapped in the ruins of a devastated hotel in London, Jet refused to move for twelve hours until the woman was reached by the rescuers.

*

It is one thing for animals to show solidarity with warring humans, and to help as porters or rescuers or bomb-sniffers. It is quite another for animals to become combatants: to use their teeth, claws or hoofs as weapons, or to intimidate (as at the Nazi concentration camps and death camps, and the prisons at Guantánamo Bay and Abu Ghraib), or to act as police attack dogs, trained to bring down suspects. Some object to these uses on the grounds of unnaturalness. The natural instinct of dogs is to enter into alliances with humans, and though loyalty to the person or property of one human might mean an attitude of occasional aggression to another human, to raise a dog whose whole purpose is to damage a member of the species with which dogs evolved seems to many to cross a dangerous line. It is taking a good instinct – that of loyalty and obedience – and twisting it to become its opposite in relation to some humans. Dogs had been known for millennia in Central and South America before the Spanish conquerors arrived. The Spaniards' dogs – a race prompted by evolution and instinct to be friendly – became a byword in the indigenous languages for oppression, dispossession and empire. That is a particular type of obscenity.

Pit bulls are regularly in the news. They sometimes do horrific damage. Yet the public outrage at the maulings is far greater than that generated by other comparable personal injury. Part of the outrage is upset at the perversion of the old dog–human relationship. We're protesting at the violation of an ancient and important propriety.

War, like most trials, makes us more visible to ourselves than we are in happier times. So we are animal lovers, are we? Well, indeed we are. There is no reason to doubt it. But the *nature* of that love and what it reveals about us are not always clear.

It might help to know that Russia, in the Second World War, created canine Molotov cocktails – dogs heavy with explosives, which were detonated when the dogs were under Nazi tanks. It might help to know that Dr Dolittle was born in the trenches of the Great War. His creator, Hugh Lofting, was disgusted by the suffering of the animals he saw there. 'To give them the same care as the men they served', he wrote, 'to develop a horse surgery … would necessitate a knowledge of horse language' – knowledge which Lofting duly gave to his most famous character. It might help to know that a significant proportion of military animals suffer life-changing PTSD after being in a combat zone. It might help to know that at the start of World War II the British government advised the evacuation of London's animals, and suggested that if they could not be evacuated they should be killed. They were, in huge numbers. In the first four days of the war about a quarter of all London's cats and dogs died – perhaps 750,000 in all. Battersea Dogs' Home became a death factory, electrocuting one hundred dogs an hour. There were stinking mounds of them in the streets. It might help to know that dachshunds, being symbols of Germany, were stoned to death in First World War Britain.[9]

Animals, whether or not they are the 'official' animals of a state or a region, are nonetheless potent political players. In the United Kingdom the royal corgis are far more tightly woven into the fabric of the nation – far more constitutionally important – than any prime minister. Garfield suggests a reason. The corgis, he thinks, 'normalized their humans; they hinted at responsibility; they enabled a show of emotion that the royal family had spent many generations repressing'. A royal who doted on her dog and wept when it died was vulnerable, accessible and affectionate, but without being un-dignifiably un-royal.[10]

The corgis did other royal work too. The surgeon David Nott, recently returned from Aleppo, found himself sitting beside the late Queen Elizabeth at lunch. When she asked him about his work, he recalled the horrors of Syria, and was too overwrought to speak. The queen asked for a box of dog biscuits, and together, for the rest of the lunch, she and Nott fed the dogs under the table while the queen chatted about the dogs. 'There', she said. 'That's so much better than talking, isn't it?'[11] The corgis here weren't enabling a display of royal emotion, but created a space for real human encounter as no other type of diplomacy could have done.

Animals are more eloquent than speeches or policies, and animal owners are more electable. During their presidential campaigns, Franklin Roosevelt, Richard Nixon, Ronald Reagan and Elizabeth Warren made sure that they were regularly photographed with their pets, and Marine Le Pen tried to soften her image by posting pictures of her kittens on her blog. 'Voters cannot get enough of dogs', said the *Boston Globe*, commenting on the prominence of Warren's golden retriever Bailey (the campaign sold 'Bailey for First Dog' handkerchiefs, for instance) and the *Globe* cited a Democratic PR adviser who said that a dog 'humanizes, if you will, a candidate. Because we say that dogs are good judges of character.' We say, half-jokingly, that dogs can detect evil. When we're voting the joke is suspended, and we wholly believe it.

The US presidency may have slipped out of Mitt Romney's hands when it emerged that he had taken his dog on holiday in a crate on the car roof. The American politician Pete Buttigieg had a campaign ad, 'Pete and Dogs', showing him cuddling and being endorsed by dogs, and announced that the affection of one particular dog showed that the dog understood 'the true meaning of patriotism'. He created Twitter accounts for his own dogs, Truman and Buddy, which disgorged political messages in their names and in the style of what the *New York Times* said were 'approximations of the sort of things Midwestern dogs might say, if they actually said anything'.[12] It was shrewd. People trust people with pets. And pet-lessness can create damaging suspicion. When Cherie Blair, on moving into 10 Downing Street, was thought (wrongly) to have banished Humphrey, the Cabinet Office cat, the great British public was not impressed. Theodore Roosevelt's happy White House, from 1901 to 1909, contained a Shetland pony (which travelled in the lift), a badger called Josiah, a bear, and numerous guinea pigs, dogs, birds, cats and snakes. Barack Obama's dogs, Bo and Sunny, are celebrities in their own right, as was George W. Bush's Scottish terrier, Barney, who was the star of eleven government film productions and had his own website.[13] Only in the presidencies of James K. Polk, Andrew Johnson and Donald Trump has the White House been pet-free (PLATE 33).

The absence of animals is usually as negatively eloquent as their presence is positively eloquent. But their presence can be sinister too. Hitler went about in public with a pure-bred German shepherd,[14] and Publius Vedius Pollio, a Roman governor of equestrian rank in the province of Asia, kept a pool of lampreys, fed on live slaves who displeased him.[15] Tertullian insists that when the slaves were dead the lampreys were cooked immediately so that Vedius could taste the slaves himself.[16]

Animals banish pretence and delusion. They are potent egalitarians. Their greatest political contribution is as democratic levellers. When one of Charles II's dogs defecated in the royal barge, it made Samuel Pepys think that 'a King and all that belong to him are as but others are'.[17]

Animals are our mirrors in the public space and on the battlefield, just as they are at the fireside, in the bedroom, in the mortuary and at the altar. It is to the altar we go now.

SEVEN

Religion and rites of passage

How did we become modern humans, with the sort of consciousness that we see as distinctively ours? The question can be answered on many levels. Here are two.

First, we evolved from non-humans. We have non-human faces only a few pages back in our family albums. In most places today this answer is uncontroversial.

Second, we became animals. This is not as controversial as it sounds. It has a respectable place in archaeological and anthropological debate. Many would agree that if it is not *the* answer, it may well be part of the answer. It is the answer given by the South African anthropologist David Lewis Williams, who postulates that the consciousness of behaviourally modern humans (*us*) erupted into the world as a result of shamanic voyaging – perhaps helped by great physiological stress (such as dancing until we were exhausted and dehydrated) or by taking plant or fungal hallucinogens.[1] Shamans from many cultures speak of leaving their own bodies and voyaging to other worlds, or other planes of existence (perhaps represented in Upper Palaeolithic times – which is when this eruption is said to have first occurred – by a journey across a cave wall).

When in the other world, the shaman met and in some sense *became* a spirit animal, and from the vantage point of that animal and that other world was able to look back at his or her body, still lying in the everyday world, and say, with new perspective and new understanding, *That is me!* The animal, in other words, gave the shaman their subjectivity: the ability to use personal pronouns meaningfully: knowledge of *self*. It sounds rather like the eating of the forbidden fruit in the Garden. That gave the knowledge of good and evil, and perhaps one cannot have such knowledge without a fully formulated self. As we've seen, the eating was instigated by an animal – the serpent.

Animal–human hybrids are depicted in Upper Palaeolithic art. Lewis Williams and others suggest that these might portray the shaman in the process of transforming to or from the animal shape. Hybrids are everywhere in subsequent mythologies: think of jackal-headed Anubis or crocodile-headed Sobek in ancient Egypt; elephant-headed Ganesha in Hinduism; Circe transforming Odysseus' men to pigs; Athena turning Arachne into a spider; Demeter turning Ascalabus into a lizard; Apuleius' Lucius becoming a donkey in *The Golden Ass* (later emulated by Bottom in *A Midsummer Night's Dream*); Gunnhild, in the Icelandic Sagas, who could turn herself into a bird; Blodeuwedd, in *The Mabinogion*, who becomes an owl; the Celtic tradition of selkies, seals who become human women – and many, many more. Shape-shifting, according to the fairy tales of all times and all places, is as characteristic of humans as bipedalism.

We can generalize these observations: we need animals not only to understand ourselves – to appreciate our historical and ecological context – but to *be* ourselves.

The Judaeo-Christian tradition, remembering the insistence, in those early chapters of Genesis, of the boundaries between categories (such as light and darkness, land and sea, human and non-human), and keen to retain the notion of human specialness, tended to frown on these stories. 'Thou shalt not suffer a witch to live', roars the book of Exodus.[2] Witches were the shamans: the shuttlers between worlds: the transgressors of those frontiers: the shape-shifters who, in Europe, often had familiars – typically cats, with whom they had a theologically dubious relationship involving the exchange of bodily forms. And so, for having a relationship with the natural world, which, for most of our human history, we all had, witches were indeed not suffered to live. For displaying the basic Darwinian and ecological truths that humans are in an unbroken continuity with, and are crucially entangled with, the non-human world, thousands of witches and far more merely suspected witches dangled from ropes and went up in smoke. Pet ownership was sometimes deadly. Even *suspected* pet ownership could kill. The Knights Templar were accused of kissing a black cat's bottom during their blasphemous services: the cat was the devil in disguise. Some think that the heterodox Cathars, who provoked the bloody Albigensian crusade, took their name from 'cat'.[3]

Yet there has always been a prominent strand of Christian thought emphasizing the immanence of God in the created order. It is more visible and audible in Eastern Christianity. 'What is a merciful heart?' asked the seventh-century saint Isaac the Syrian. 'It is a heart on fire for the whole of creation, for humankind, for the birds, for the animals, for the demons, for all that exists.' The Greek Orthodox morning prayer includes the words 'Holy Spirit, giver of life, present in all places and filling all things…' 'All places' and 'all things' includes dogs, cats, gerbils and snakes.

It was from this strand that the famous theology of St Francis was woven. He tamed the man-killing wolf of Gubbio, in a recapitulation of the domestication of wolves by hunter–gatherers, and his 1225 song 'The Canticle of the Sun' (arguably the first poem in vernacular

Italian – appropriate for a poem celebrating things that spring up out of the earth) begins:

> Most High, all-powerful, good Lord,
> Yours are the praises, the glory, the honour, and all blessings.
> To You alone, Most High, do they belong,
> and no man is worthy to mention Your name.
> Praised be You, my Lord, with all your creatures…

It continues, in a passage emphasizing the goodness rather than the corruption of the non-human world:

> Praised be You, my Lord, through Sister Mother Earth,
> who sustains us and governs us and who produces
> varied fruits with coloured flowers and herbs.[4]

None of this would surprise many other religious traditions – indeed 'The Canticle' bears a striking resemblance to the Hindu *Gayatri mantra* – nor vibrantly ecocentric Celtic Christianity. In the seventh century, St Cuthbert of Lindisfarne, after praying all night, submerged in the sea (not penitentially, because he thought the cold would be good for his soul, but so that he could feel literally embraced by the non-human world), was warmed and dried on the beach by otters. The otters were not pets, but if he could forge a connection like that with wild animals, it must have been wondrous to behold his rapport with a dog. There are, too, many instances in the Judaeo-Christian scriptures of a connection between humans and animals other than one in which we eat them (think, for instance, of Elijah being fed by the ravens, or of the great fish in the Jonah story – probably not a whale – being used as an instrument of divine discipline). Jesus repeatedly used agricultural stories to make his point – stories such as the tale of the lost sheep (an animal for whom the shepherd had a more-than-commercial regard), and referred to himself as the Lamb of God.[5]

Christopher Smart, confined for insanity in St Luke's Hospital, Bethnal Green, between 1759 and 1763, famously considered his cat Jeoffry, concluding that Jeoffry was

> …the servant of the Living God duly and daily serving him.
> For at the first glance of the glory of God in the East
> he worships in his Way.
> For this is done by wreathing his body seven times round
> with elegant quickness.
> For then he leaps up to catch the musk, which is the blessing
> of God upon his prayer…[6]

Despite these connections, and despite the central part that animals play in human lives, minds and history, animals have tended to be sidelined in the liturgies of the mainstream Christian denominations. Look hard, though, and they are there.

Roman Catholicism has its own patron saint of animals, St Anthony of Egypt, who has a particular fondness for pigs. He blessed and healed a sick piglet, which became his constant companion, and on the feast day of St Francis services are held for the blessing of companion animals. The Eastern Orthodox *Book of Needs* has prayers for the health of donkeys, horses, mules, cattle, sheep, bees and silkworms – though it must be admitted that the emphasis in these intercessions is on getting them back to being economically productive – a telling emphasis.[7]

In countless churches across the world there are special days in which animals are sprinkled with holy water, thanked and commended to the care of God, and a corps of specialist animal chaplains has arisen to usher animals under the protective wings of God.

Perhaps the world's biggest (and probably loudest) St Francis' Day celebration is at the St John the Divine Church in Morningside, New York, which regularly has five hundred animals, including rats, cockroaches, raptors, fennec foxes, goats, alpacas, camels and elephants.[8]

Britain, so far, is more modest, but is heading in that direction. In a recent survey, 63 per cent of 285 British churches said that they welcomed dogs or held pet services. St Botolph's, Boston, Lincolnshire, has been designated an 'Animal Friendly Church' and offers snacks and a 'warm welcome to visiting dogs'. Dogs, apparently, are 'also attending bell ringing events' (can they really enjoy them, with hearing as acute as theirs?) and being 'increasingly catered to with refreshments, special treats, events and walking trails'.[9] More than half of England's cathedrals welcome, or at least tolerate, dogs.[10] Not during services, though, which is a break from tradition. Commonly, at least until the seventeenth century, pets, being part of the home, attended church with the rest of the household, from master and mistress to scullery maid, and today, throughout Africa, Asia and Latin America, dogs, cats and chickens wander unmolested round churches while the service is on. It's logical enough: why should any part of the household be unblessed? One vicar, justifying the dog-friendliness of her church, emphasized that 'For many people, dogs are their only day to day companion and an important part of their family.'[11] Bless the dog, bless the person; bless the person, bless the dog. They're not really distinct entities.

Animals are more prominently present in many non-Christian traditions. Take Tihar, for instance – an annual Hindu festival celebrated particularly in Nepal. The second day, Kukur Tihar, recalls the story of Yudhishthira, one of the main protagonists of the *Mahabharata*, who (reminding us of the child and the proto-dog in the Chauvet cave) refuses to enter the celestial home of the *devas* unless accompanied by a dog. The dog turns out to be the god Yama. On Kukur Tihar, Yama-in the-dog is worshipped. Dogs, both strays and beloved house dogs, are garlanded, fed treats, and the *tika* mark placed on their foreheads.[12]

The temple of Deshnoke, in Rajasthan, is dedicated to the goddess Karni Mata. She chose to be incarnate as a rat, and when her human descendants die they will be reincarnated as rats. About 20,000 rats live in the temple, swarming over devotees and visitors and eating from the same plates. They are not just tolerated, but welcomed. For worshippers at the temple, to share a chapati with a rat is to host a revered ancestor.[13] A Jewish ceremony for the blessing of animals is often held on the seventh day of Passover, when Jews remember the escape of the Hebrews and their animals from their bondage in Egypt.[14] Unsurprisingly, animal blessings in Judaism occur too after the reading of the story of Noah's Ark. The theology of these timings is similar: animals and humans are bound inextricably together. It's very *ecological*. In the story of the Exodus humans and animals are both refugees. In the story of Noah humans and animals are literally in the same boat. Looking at animals reminds us of our own predicament. Animals, yet again, tell us about ourselves.

We share with our animals, and our animals companionably share with us, mortality, contingency and suffering. We may seek to make our animals more like ourselves so that they can share more of life's burdens. This may be behind apparent kindnesses to our animals, and behind bizarre rituals such as the Bark Mitzvah, (seen as blasphemous by some), a coming-of-age ceremony for a dog, in which the dog may wear a yarmulke and be draped in a prayer shawl. It began as pastiche, in Beverly Hills, of course, but nothing is ever completely ridiculous, and the Bark Mitzvah is a serious sign of the conflation of human and pet interests. 'A Bark Mitzvah is more than just a quirky celebration', says a dog rehoming charity. 'This unique event provides an opportunity to create lasting memories and celebrate the unconditional love, loyalty and joy that dogs bring into our lives.... [G]ive your furry companion a celebration they'll always remember.' 'It's a testament to the deep bond between humans and their beloved dogs.'[15]

Just as in the other cases we've seen where humans make liturgical movements, ostensibly for the benefit of animals, the Bark Mitzvah is really for the benefit of humans: it is to bind the animals closer to us so that they can shoulder more of our angst. In the real Bar or Bat Mitzvah the Jewish child celebrates their coming of age and becomes personally responsible for keeping the Law. In the Bark Mitzvah the dog becomes responsible for our happiness.

*

Every year the United Kingdom has a National Pet Month. The idea started in 1989, as National Pet Week, but it was obviously decided that we now have four times as much need for whatever it is that Pet Week gave us.

Pet Month has its own 'Order for a Pets' Service', entitled 'One of the Family'. It reminds us that in times past people took their dogs to church, where 'straw mixed with rosemary was often placed on the floor, and incense would have sweetened the air'. (It primly doesn't remind us why it was necessary for incense to sweeten the air.) 'Humans, like animals', we're told, 'have senses and when all our senses are engaged in worship we are most truly ourselves before God.' That's interesting. Dogs and cats are far more sensorily switched on than we are, and, if the Order of Service is correct, the more we are like our dogs and cats (at least in that respect), the more properly human we will be. Humans, made in the image of God, will presumably conform more closely to that image if they refashion themselves in the likeness of a Jack Russell.

What is the service for, other than to encourage you to become more like your dog and hence more acceptable to God? It is 'a wonderful opportunity to thank God for the gift of animals, and for us to ask God's blessing on all that he has made'. A blessing, we're told, 'involves praise of God; the wish that spiritual good fortune will go with what is blessed and dedicates someone or something for a sacred purpose. A blessing also reminds us that all good gifts are gifts from God.' After the first hymn (it doesn't specify what that hymn is, but it must inevitably be 'All Things Bright and Beautiful')[16] the liturgy continues:

> God called us in the beginning to be stewards of His creation, caring for and nurturing the world He made. As we come to ask for God's blessing on our pets we first ask for forgiveness for the times we have not made the best use of His blessings and gifts.

No guidance is given about the specific pet-related shortcomings of which we should repent (I can think of a few likely candidates), but once the congregation has repented of whatever it is, it is time for the Thanksgiving:

> We thank you for giving us these pets who bring us joy. As you take care of us, we also ask that we might take care of those who trust us to look after them. By doing this, we share in your own love for all creation.[17]

It's another interesting formulation. Pets have been given to us by God, and by appreciating the gift, and caring for our pets as God cares for us, we become, hopefully, more loving towards the whole created order. Pets, then, are a divinely ordained device for increasing our general benevolence. And since to be benevolent is to be more consonant with our true divine image, pets help us to be more authentically human. We're coming to the same conclusion from many different directions.

Though these events are true balm for many, they are a gift to a comedian. There are many practical tips offered by experienced practitioners. 'Think about waste/cleaning' suggests one. 'This is usually not a problem, but some congregations prefer to hold their blessings outside just in case.'[18] 'Try to keep different types of animals a bit separate for the safety of all', advises another. 'Safety must be paramount – the worst possible outcome would be for someone to go home with an injured pet! Small animals like rabbits, mice, guinea pigs etc. are usually best left in their cages for protection. If you are lucky enough to have a python brought along, make sure that children do not pat food animals like mice before patting the snake (to avoid bitten fingers).'[19]

★

We've visited in this book ceremonies in which humans are the notional officiants, and suggested that animals might be doing the real spiritual work there. Sometimes the pets are the priests.

In St Johnsbury, Vermont, artist and author Stephen Huneck built a Dog Chapel on Dog Mountain, a 150 acre estate. In his words, it is a 'place where people can go and celebrate the spiritual bond they have with their dogs'. It has become a memorial chapel, its walls encrusted with drawings, letters, photos and keepsakes, but equally important, says Huneck, is 'celebrating the joy of living' with their pets (PLATE 37). The pews are supported by carved, painted dogs. The stained-glass windows show scenes from the life of a black Labrador, and each window has a theme: Peace, Play, Joy, Friend, Trust, Faith and Love. There is no altar; just a rug depicting two Labradors playing tug o' war.

Gail Gilmore's dog, Chispa, was diagnosed with canine cognitive dysfunction. Treatments failed, and the dog's condition deteriorated. Gail, deeply distressed, was drawn to the Dog Chapel. A dog called Annie was there, and licked Gail's face and hands. Gail felt

> a rush of what I can only describe as the purest form of love sweep through my body … although I want to share my belief that the soul of one of my own dogs, dead now for nearly nine years, reached out to me through Annie, I stop just short of doing so.

> The feeling of resurrection that's come from my interaction with Annie feels too personal, too impossible to articulate. I've been touched by God in this place, and I know it. Out of nowhere, a silent prayer for her takes shape in my mind: May you live a long and happy life, may you be comforted as you have comforted others, and may the unconditional love you give with such joy come back to you over and over, now and forever. Amen.[20]

Annie was the priest; the mediator; the celebrant. Or possibly the sacrament. Others have spoken about animals that way. Sometimes animals have been a bridgehead to the gods by being sacrificed for them. Sometimes – for instance in the mythology of ancient Egypt – animal-headed gods, such as the jackal or jackal-headed Anubis, help to conduct the deceased to another world.[21] In the literature of mediaeval Europe, getting lost in the pursuit of a white hart is a well-recognized avenue to mystical experience.

More mundanely, Julie Castaneda, who runs a doggy daycare facility in Topeka, Kansas, started to take her charges out for walks on a Sunday morning, and then wrote devotional Facebook posts about how her experiences with the dogs made her feel closer to God. The posts turned into a book.[22] Who preaches on those Sunday mornings? Castaneda is clear: 'If unconditional love is the lesson we have to learn, then dogs are our greatest teachers.' She has 'captured how we can connect to the Divine through our four-legged friends', wrote one reviewer.[23] The High Priest of Amun at Thebes would want to add some explanatory footnotes, but he would 'Like' the review.

Animals were there when we became behaviourally modern humans. They may have had a central part in that process – and, if so, it was an explicitly 'spiritual' process, involving the relocation of a soul into the body of another animal. They are there at our other spiritual and religious moments: watching in the paintings as saints are born, looking on from rood screens and stained-glass windows as we are baptised and married, generating a sense of holy calm as homemakers, showing divine loyalty when every human lets us down, wagging their tails and slinking through Bible readings and along the margins of illuminated manuscripts. They are there too, as we will see in Chapter 8, at and after our deaths, and may give there even more comfort than they gave us when they walked at our side round the block.

They are at, and may *be*, the crucial rites of passage. They are symbols of our childhood innocence, yet by them we were introduced to death. Unlike our parents, they understood us when we went through the trials of puberty. Buying a dog by oneself may be today, in our economically straitened world, the modern equivalent of leaving one's parents: a declaration of independence. They are the only ones who will not judge our crow's feet and greying hair. They give a kind of absolution from time. They help to hush the neuroses which stop us being us.

St Isaac the Syrian, writing about the business of domestication, said:

> The humble person approaches the wild animals, and the moment they catch sight of him their ferocity is tamed. They come up and cling to him as to their master, wagging their tails and licking his hands and feet. For they smell on him the same smell that came from Adam before the transgression.[24]

For St Isaac, domestication – or at least harmony between humans and animals – is what happens when human beings are being what humans really are.

EIGHT

Their ends and ours: death and beyond

The importance of animals as companions is in sharpest focus when we lose them, by death or otherwise. Only then, perhaps, do we really know what they have meant.

Walter Scott was devoted to Abbotsford, his house in the Scottish borders, and was devastated when it seemed he would be forced to sell it. But there was something more troubling still:

> the thoughts of parting from these dumb creatures [the pets he had accumulated] have moved me more than any of the painful reflections I have put down – poor things, I must get them kind masters.... I must end this, or I shall lose the tone of mind with which men should meet distress.[1]

Samuel Pepys similarly worried that his lost dog had stripped him of the poise with which a dignified man should meet tragedy:

> [A]fter dinner, by water towards Woolwich, and in our way I bethought myself that we had left our poor little dog that followed us out of doors at the waterside, and God knows whether he be not lost, which did not only strike my wife into a great passion but I must confess myself also; more than was becoming me.[2]

Non-human animals, it seems, can dehumanize humans precisely *because* they can humanize us. It's as if the animal becomes entangled with a vital part of the human, and when the animal is ripped away, so is a defining element of humanity. We've seen that pet animals create ecosystems. When the pet dies, it's not *just* the pet who dies: an ecosystem tumbles. There will be no more chats with the fellow dog walkers; no more peering into the top of hedges from the back of the horse; no more reason to get up before dawn to manicure the cat for triumph at the cat show; no acute nose to tell you what the local foxes have been doing in the night; no whirring of the hamster wheel to keep you company when you wake in the early hours; no twittering from the cage in the corner of the room to remind you of the birds in the African plains from which our ancestors come.

Consistently, when owners are asked to name the main downside of having a pet, they list not the cost, the allergies, the risk of being savaged, or the burden of clearing up faeces, but the trauma of the animal's death.

We saw in Chapter 4, in Catullus' words, how devoted Lesbia was to her pet sparrow. The devotion was ultimately the cause of great pain. Here is Catullus again, describing Lesbia's devastation at the sparrow's death:

> Mourn, Venuses and Cupids,
> and all the charming lovers that there are!
> My darling's sparrow is dead,
> the sparrow that was my darling's delight,
> whom she loved more than her very eyes;
> for he was honey-sweet, and knew his mistress
> as well as a girl knows her own mother.
> Nor would he move from her lap,
> but hopping about now here, now there,
> used to chirrup constantly to his mistress alone.
> Now he goes along that gloomy road,
> from where they say no one returns.
> But a curse upon you, accursed shades
> of Orcus, which devour all lovely things!

Such a pretty sparrow you have stolen away.
What a cruel deed! Alas, poor little bird!
Because of you my darling's eyes
are heavy and red with weeping. [3]

When Anne Boleyn's tiny dog Purkoy was killed in a fall, her courtiers, knowing how shattering the news would be, did not dare to tell her. Henry VIII had to tell her instead. It is hard to think of him as a sympathetic pet bereavement counsellor.

Wordsworth wept as he buried his dog Little Music at the foot of an oak tree, Abraham Lincoln was appalled when his pet pig was slaughtered, and when Walter Scott's bull terrier Camp died in 1809 he noted that the short lives of beloved animals might, curiously, be a kind of mercy: 'If we suffer so in losing a dog after an acquaintance of ten or twelve years, what would it be if they were to live double that time?'

It says a lot that this terrible trauma is thought to be outweighed by the benefit of the life. The author Simon Garfield, contemplating the death of his Labrador, Ludo, realizes that he cherishes even Ludo's 'warm but lightly offensive pungency', and, though relieved that he will no longer have to pay more than £1,000 per year in insurance, comments: 'Goodness knows how we'll cope when he dies.'[4]

We try just about anything, including penury, to pay the vet bills and keep the ecosystem running, but eventually we have to accept that the end is near.

★

Human end-of-life care is recognized as a medical specialty, and care for animals at the end of their lives is increasingly seen as demanding special skills too.

Alexis Fleming founded what she believes to be the first animal hospice, the Maggie Fleming Animal Hospice (named after her dog

Maggie), in south-west Scotland. She looks after just three animals at a time, so that each can get intense and individual care. Speaking of one inmate, she said:

> his latest blood results show he is starting to slip into liver and kidney dysfunction. I sit with him for a couple of hours each day, washing his face with a warm cloth, which he loves, and giving him a massage to ease his muscles. I have promised him that when he tells me it is time to go I will listen. I will be there on his last day with all his favourite things and hold him as he slips away peacefully, knowing someone loved him to the last.[5]

There are now, too, specialist veterinary euthanasists. Dr Suzen Gregersen is a veterinary surgeon who runs Vets2Home – 'Peaceful Pet Goodbyes' – an at-home pet euthanasia service. She explains that she and the other vets in her team never dreamt, when they started their careers, that they would spend most of their professional lives ending animal lives. But she is passionate about her mission:

> One thing we do know for sure, after helping thousands of pets find peace, is a loving goodbye is so much better when done at home, with loving pet parents or family gathered around in the favourite, familiar spot. The 'secret' is having time to give that tailored, gentle but deep sedation first. We call this end, 'the blessed sleep', the sleep that ends all suffering and grants the 'gift of peace' when it is most needed. This is why and how we do what we do: For the love of animals and for them to find peace, at home when this 'last resort' is the last loving gesture we can do for them.[6]

Pet owners have traditionally coped with their bereavement by using ritual and theology. We will look later in this chapter at theological coping mechanisms, which include belief in the eternal soul of the departed pet. First, though, a look at rituals, with a view to seeing what they tell us about our real view of our pets.

When Evelyn Waugh wrote *The Loved One* (1948), featuring a Californian pet funeral service and its cemetery 'The Happier Hunting Ground', he meant it as satire. The 'Grade A service' included 'several unique features. At the moment of committal, a white dove, symbolizing the deceased's soul, is liberated over the crematorium.'

Since pets were individuals, their departures were bespoke: '[O]ne [customer] after filling half the icebox for over a week with a dead she-bear changed her mind and called in the taxidermist', and there was

> the ritualistic, almost orgiastic cremation of a non-sectarian chimpanzee and the burial of a canary over whose tiny grave a squad of Marine buglers had sounded Taps. It is forbidden by Californian law to scatter human remains from an aeroplane, but the sky is free to the animal world and on one occasion it fell to Dennis to commit the ashes of a tabby-cat to the slip-stream over Sunset Boulevard.

Though the choreography varied, the significance of the animal's life was unvaryingly affirmed, and seen as comparable to our own:

> In the presence of a dozen mourners the coffin of an Alsatian was lowered into the flower-lined tomb. The Reverend Errol Bartholomew read the service. 'Dog that is born of bitch hath but a short time to live, and is full of misery. He cometh up, and is cut down like a flower; he fleeth as it were a shadow…'[7]

Read today, though, it is not satire at all, but simple reportage, prophecy and history. There is a pet funeral industry worth millions of pounds.

The services offered by Dignity Pet Crematorium are typical. So are their pitches, both negative and positive. The negative:

> The sad truth is that not much has changed in the pet cremation services offered by veterinary practices over the past 20 years. The standard 'ashes back' service still means most pets will be taken

away each week alongside the vets' clinical waste with no special handling and the majority of 'communal' cremations are simple disposal operations where remains are taken to landfill sites afterwards.

The message: your pet is special. It is tantamount to a human relative or friend, and you wouldn't sling your grandmother into a landfill site, would you?

They promise 'to treat your pet with the utmost care and respect', 'to cremate your pet individually', to ensure that the ashes you receive 'are only those of your pet', and 'to personalise the service for you'.

They charge by weight, up to a point. The standard cremation of a St Bernard, a Bernese Mountain Dog or a Deerhound will set you back £285, a cat £180, a hamster or budgie £90, a medium tortoise (8–10 inches) £130, a hedgehog £95, a bearded dragon £95, a rat £85, a corn snake £95 and a goldfish £70, but there are many optional extras, including urns and caskets and 'keepsakes and memorials'. You might opt for a 'Crystal Tealight Candle Holder Urn' (£90–110), which 'will hold a segment or a lock of hair' in the silver or gold cylinder and is 'crowned with a beautiful Swarovski crystal element', or a 'Hanging Pet Memorial Slate' with photo and original paw print (£55). A 'Bluebell Scatter Tube' for the ashes (£10–20, depending on size) is 'ideal for scattering or burying your pet's ashes'. For £145 you can 'put your pet's paw or nose print on a stunning 20 mm solid silver keyring', which will allow you to 'keep the pet you love most close to you at all times' and a 'miniature urn key ring' (£20) lets you have 'a token amount of your pet's ashes or fur' always in your pocket. A hamster-shaped casket (£39, available in bronze and black) has a compartment for the ashes and a lock of hair. It is 'the perfect resting place for your beloved hamster', and will help in 'cherishing lasting memories'. A CD of Rachel Fuller's 'Animal Requiem', 'to celebrate and honour the animals that we have loved and lost', recorded with the Royal Philharmonia, and featuring Alfie Boe and Paul McCartney, costs £15.

A horse is more expensive in both life and death. A cremation for a medium-sized horse costs £1,150, including collection within 30 miles, and deposition of the ashes in a 'rustic and sturdy' casket – 'a charming and discreet way' to hold the ashes, which is 'double sealed to make sure the ashes stay safe' above the 'memento tray' – for rosettes, shoes, mane or tail clippings.

I do not mock. The testimonials are moving, and show that bereaved owners are genuinely comforted. Pet bereavement can be devastating, and may be particularly acute where the owner has made the decision to have the animal put to sleep.

'Michael Field', the pen name used by a pair of English poets, Katharine Harris Bradley and Edith Emma Cooper, filled a manuscript book with memorial poems celebrating the life and death of their dog Whym Chow: *Whym Chow: Flame of Love* (PLATE 28). They evidently had the dog euthanized. One poem, 'My Cup', is plainly an attempt to come to terms with their guilt.[8]

Chow, thou hast drunk the bitter Cup –
Love unto death,
That makes love free and lifts it up
To heaven and its own breath:
So God gave death
To His Beloved, as we
Gave it to thee.
Oh, 'twas a sacramental cup –
Death given for Love!
We bade thy little spirit sup
With First and Last above,
When of our love
We made thee free
Eternally.[9]

Here the vet is God's proxy, giving death to God's beloved. Over a century later, the poems have moved online, but the gist is the same.

An Instagram search for #petloss produces hundreds of thousands of posts. The actress Kate Beckinsale described online her devastation when her cat Clive died. 'My heart is absolutely and totally broken', she wrote. She celebrated his life with a shoulder tattoo, wondering 'How can a light that burned so brightly, suddenly burn so pale.'[10]

Some 85 per cent of pet owners report loss and grief symptoms like those caused by the loss of a human family member. A third are still grieving six months after the death, and almost a quarter a year on.[11] The internet is awash with support services, and they are well and increasingly used. Cruse, a bereavement charity primarily directed at people who have lost human relatives, links from their pet bereavement page to the human page dealing with 'Ways to remember someone who has died', which suggests creating a photo collage, making a memory box, planting a tree or dedicating a bench in the name of the deceased, making something out of their old clothing, organizing an event in their honour, donating to a charity that was important to them, learning to play their favourite song, writing them a letter, visiting a place that was special to them, making their favourite food, making a video montage, having something of theirs repaired, and speaking to people who knew them.

None of this would have been a surprise to the Egyptians of the Sixth Dynasty (2345–2181 BCE), who buried a greyhound-like dog called Abuwtiyuw (which might be an onomatopoeic name mimicking his bark – or more likely, to my ear, his howl) near the Great Pyramid of Giza. His body has not been found, but his memorial stone has, and it shows the same concern for the post-mortem dignity of a dog shown today by those who buy Swarovski-crystal caskets. 'The dog which was the guard of His Majesty, Abuwtiyuw is his name', the stone reads.

> His Majesty ordered that he be buried [ceremonially], that he be given a coffin from the royal treasury, fine linen in great quantity, [and] incense. His Majesty [also] gave perfumed ointment, and [ordered] that a tomb be built for him by the gangs of masons. His Majesty did this for him in order that he [the dog] might be Honoured [before the great god, Anubis].[12]

There are many other instances of respectful animal burials, from prehistory onwards – though it is not always clear what they signify. Some, as we will see, denote the animal's importance in proclaiming the identity and status of the dead human, rather than signifying simple affection. But when Alexander's beloved dog Peritas died, and was buried as a hero, the burial was an assertion of friendship, and so, surely, was the interment in fourth-century BC Athens of a dog with a lamp to light his way through the underworld and a beef bone to keep him going on the journey. Many of the numerous Roman pet graves speak of intimate companionship and the pain of bereavement. The epitaph of Pearl, a first- or second-century lapdog from Gaul, reads:

> I used to lie on the soft lap of my master and mistress
> and knew to go to bed when tired on my spread mattress
> and I did not speak more than allowed as a dog, given a silent mouth
> No-one was scared by my barking.

Others are more fulsome – and more mysterious. The grave stele of 'Helena' (150–200 CE), depicts only a dog (PLATE 2). The inscription refers to Helena as 'our foster-daughter' or 'nurseling', an 'incomparable and well-deserving soul'. Was Helena a dog or a girl? Views differ.

And so it continues through the ages. Ercole Strozzi, in the late fifteenth or early sixteenth century CE, penned a 213-line elegy to the dog Borgettus (the pet of the humanist poet Antonio Tebaldeo).[13] It was one of many elegies, by many poets, on this doubtless worthy but overcelebrated dog. Strozzi's elegy was rivalled by Francesco

Beccuti's sixteenth-century celebration of the life and death of a beloved cat, whose eyes were represented in the heavens by two new and dazzling stars.[14] My favourite pet epitaph is the laconic inscription in a Lancashire pet cemetery: 'Rex: 14 years of pleasure and fun / Ended by a hit and run' (PLATE 39).[15]

Cats sometimes had less honourable mentions in memorial poems. The cat Gyb, for instance, killed John Skelton's pet sparrow Philip, prompting an outpouring of grief in *The Boke of Phyllyp Sparowe*:

> For the sowle of Philip Sparowe,
> That was late slayn at Carowe,
> Among the Nones Blake,
> For that swete soules sake,
> And for all sparowes soules,
> Set in our bederolles,
> Pater noster qui,
> With an Ave Mari.[16]

★

The shrewd nineteenth century saw that there was money to be made from these ancient and ubiquitous sentiments. And so we have the first commercial pet cemeteries. (Earlier cemeteries, such as the gigantic Bronze Age dog cemetery at Ashkelon, near the Gaza Strip, have different origins. We will return to them.)

England's first pet cemetery was established by the Duchess of York in the grounds of Oakland House in Surrey. Sixty dogs are interred there. The first (notionally) egalitarian cemetery was on the northern edge of Hyde Park, and had around three hundred dead guests. It is dwarfed by the Cimetière des Chiens in Paris, which has more than 40,000, which in turn looks small beside Hartsdale Canine Cemetery, Westchester County, New York, which was founded in 1896, and hosts more than 70,000.

We have seen that we increasingly give our pets the time, money and moral status of humans. We feed them on human food, drape them in jewels, invite them into our beds, give them the medical care we would like to have ourselves, and bury them with the sacred obsequies we give to our relatives.

Yet all this is something of an understatement.

Lord Byron's Newfoundland dog, Boatswain, died of rabies, and is buried in the Hyde Park pet cemetery. The inscription on the memorial stone was composed by Sir John Hobhouse:

> Near this Spot
> Are deposited the Remains of one
> who possessed Beauty without Vanity,
> Strength without Insolence
> Courage without Ferocity,
> and all the virtues of Man without his Vices.

Boatswain was not just morally equivalent to a human: he was *better.* 'Four legs good, two legs bad' chanted the animals in *Animal Farm.* We're starting to agree.

★

If we have lived what we consider to be a good life, a good death is one concordant with that life. We like to die where we have lived – both physically and metaphorically: at home, in the nexus of the relationships that have constituted and supported us. That, for many, means dying in the bosom of our pets.

As one English hospice wrote,

> We regularly have visits from our little four-legged friends and they bring lots of joy. Recently we had a family at the hospice who brought their treasured cat in to see their dad. He curled up on his bed and helped the whole family relax at the hospice. We currently have a beautiful little dog with a patient, helping him feel like he was at home. It has helped him settle at the hospice and enabled him to feel comfortable enough to stay for pain management and then when he's ready he will go back home.

> Would you believe we even arranged for a patient to see her horse one last time. It was her final wish and we were able to make that happen for her.[17]

'Getting to see, touch, pet and hold their beloved pets again can be an enormous mood-booster to hospice patients and can even temporarily improve their health', commented a hospice chain in the United States.

> Visits can be helpful to the pet too, as they undoubtedly have been missing their owner. Because you cannot explain to a pet the circumstances surrounding their owner's health the way you can to a child about a relative, it can be sad and distressing to watch a pet continually walk around the patient's home looking for them. If the pet can see them and smell them, they can better come to terms with the situation.[18]

The emphasis here is on the healing and emollient power of relationship – from the pet to the dying person, and vice versa. This is unsurprising. If animals have comforted during life, should we not expect them to comfort all the more as life ebbs?

It is always hard and – who knows? – perhaps harder, for those left behind. The literature is full of accounts of mourning animals.

The most famous is the story of Greyfriars Bobby, a Skye terrier so devoted to his master, an Edinburgh policeman called John Gray, that when Gray died Bobby stayed by his grave for fourteen years, from 1858 to 1872, and is commemorated by a much-photographed statue.

It's a touching story, but sadly it is probably a hoax, concocted by the cemetery's curator, John Brown, and John Traill, the owner of a nearby restaurant. Bobby, thinks historian Jan Bondeson, probably never had an owner at all, but was one of many strays who frequented Edinburgh's graveyards and were fed by the groundsmen. The myth served Brown and Traill well. It lured visitors to the graveyard – where, moved by Brown's generosity in maintaining the dog, they gave him donations – and to the restaurant. Bobby, argues Bondeson, died in 1867, but was cynically replaced by a similar-looking Skye terrier to keep the money flowing.[19]

There are, though, many similar stories untouched by cynicism.

On the morning of 12 December 1953, during one the harshest ever winters in England, 85-year-old shepherd Joe Tagg set out from his home in north Derbyshire with his sheepdog, Tip, to check on his sheep. He never returned. Search parties scoured the high moors in vain until, on 27 March 1954 – fifteen weeks after Joe had gone missing – two shepherds, rounding up their sheep high on Ronksley Moor, found Joe's body lying in a dip. A few feet away, emaciated and barely alive, was Tip, who must have survived by foraging for dead animals, themselves killed by the cold. Tip's loyalty was rewarded with the Bronze Medal of the Canine Defence League.[20]

Tip's story recalls that of the young artist Charles Gough, who in 1805 went walking in the Lake District. He too never returned. Three months after his disappearance a shepherd found the body, guarded by his dog. Gough and the dog were immortalized by Wordsworth in his poem 'Fidelity':

> Yes, proof was plain that since the day
> On which the Traveller thus had died
> The Dog had watch'd about the spot,
> Or by his Master's side:
> How nourish'd here through such long time
> He knows, who gave that love sublime,
> And gave that strength of feeling, great
> Above all human estimate.

Again the trope: an animal, 'Above all human estimate', outdoes a human in human virtue.

These stories hint at some real emotional sentiment on the part of the animal, but there is room for scepticism. Were the dogs not simply doing what they were programmed to do – namely guard the physical body of their master? And, anyway, perhaps they had no real option but to stay by the bodies: perhaps they did not know the way home.

Such scepticism is harder to sustain in the cases of Fido and Hachiko. The appropriately named Fido belonged to Carlo Soriani, who was killed in an air raid in 1943. For fourteen years afterwards, Fido waited by Soriano's customary bus stop, near Florence, for his master to return. And for nine years after the death of his master, Hidesaburo Ueno, Hachiko went every evening to Shibuya station, in Japan, at exactly the right time, to meet the train on which Ueno had always travelled.

Was it just the power of habit, unleavened by, well, *love*, that propelled these dogs to the bus stop and the train station? It is hard to believe so. The dogs were holding in their minds (if they had anything akin to a mind) a memory – an abstract idea. It is more likely that some sort of affect was encrusted on this abstraction than that the dogs were icy, emotionless automata.

Dog mourning is doubtless different from ours, for their way of being is different from ours. They live mainly in a scent world, and presumably miss the smell of the deceased more than her sight. Smells, for us, often summon the past more powerfully than sight. It may be the same – or more so – for nose-led animals. They may have more potent olfactory memories than us, and may inhabit the past more intensely than we do. The smell centres are located in the most evolutionarily ancient part of our brains – the fish-brain bit. It might be said that they are more fundamental elements of us than the more recent sight centres – allied closely, as those sight centres are, to the callow neurological new kid on the block, the cerebral cortex. Dogs are at least as entwined with us as we are with them, and the wrench to their innards of our deaths might be more sickening and damaging to them than theirs (or our parents') is to us. Dogs, in other words, might grieve more painfully than us.

★

A beloved pet at our bedside won't necessarily comfort us when we're dying. If a relationship with an animal has been important during life, the prospect of being parted by death might increase the anxiety of the human patient.

There are psychologically compelling reasons to believe that death will not separate us from our animals. These reasons are accommodated by many belief systems. Just as the Upper Palaeolithic child walked more calmly with the wolf or proto-dog into the dark of the cave (see Chapter 2), so we may walk more calmly into the dark if we believe that our dog walks alongside us, or will eventually come bounding after and catch us up. Death is a lonely business, and if a dog, cat, horse or bearded dragon has mitigated loneliness in life, there is nothing more natural than to hope it will continue to do so. Remember the puppy in the Natufian burial, and the halitotic old dog alongside its owner in Carthage. We cannot know to what metaphysical scheme their owners subscribed, but that scheme surely said, however vaguely, that the owners and their dogs shared some future.

We have seen several examples of animal burials in Chapter 7 – and there are many more. When, in the *Iliad*, Patroclus was killed, he was joined on the pyre by two of his nine beloved dogs, several horses, sheep and cows, and twelve Trojan youths.[21] The late Queen Elizabeth II declared that her corgis would not long survive her death, but presumably she did not have anything like that in mind.[22]

Pliny the Younger relates how, when Regulus' son died, Regulus sacrificed his son's many ponies, his big and small dogs, and his pet nightingales, parrots and blackbirds around the funeral pyre

– presumably cremating them too. This, comments Pliny, was a rather excessive display of grief.[23] The sense is that it was rather uppity and vulgar, for the son was no Patroclus.

That's an interesting prejudice. For your cremation smoke to be mingled with the smoke of your pets was, Pliny seems to think, an aristocratic prerogative. It may follow from that that an afterlife shared with one's pets was an aristocratic privilege too.

In the Celtic world dogs were sacrificed so that they could be companions in the afterlife, and there are comparable examples from many locations, including North and South America, China and Japan. But we need not travel so far in time or space to meet the phenomenon. When Ralph Neville, First Earl of Westmorland, died in 1425, he was buried in the chancel of the little church of Staindrop, County Durham. His greyhound lay beside him.[24]

Egypt, as so often, provides some of the clearest and most exuberant illustrations.[25] In Memphis, under the temple of Anubis, the god of mummification, over 8 million mummified dogs were buried over a period of around twenty years. They had probably come from a nearby puppy farm, presumably maintained for that purpose. The companionship of dogs in the afterlife was big business.[26] It wasn't just dogs who were mummified, of course. Many other animals were too: cats, crocodiles, ibises and dung beetles amongst them. The afterlife wouldn't be the same without them.[27]

In some schemes, ancient and modern, the afterlife was *this* life, and could involve pets. Pythagoras rebuked a man who was beating a dog, saying that the dog's soul was that of Pythagoras' dead friend: 'I heard him speak', insisted Pythagoras. We modern westerners may shrink from the notion of the transmigration of souls – which of course has a respected place in Buddhism and Hinduism – but we treat our dogs as if it is true, and eat cows as if it is not.

There is not so much of a tradition of pet-keeping in India as in many other places. I wonder if Hindu beliefs about reincarnation might be partly responsible? It must be metaphysically complicated to have an animal in a cage which might be a human at some stage of a transmigratory journey.

Christianity is unusual amongst the world's religions in being able to countenance, at least officially, in some places, for a while, the idea of an animal-free afterlife. Aquinas, following Aristotle, agreed that animals had souls, but not *immortal* souls: not self-reflective or rational souls; not the sort of souls that can be saved.

By and large, Eastern Christianity has agreed. Bishop Kallistos Ware pointed out that in modern Greek 'horse' is *alogon* – lacking *logos* or reason, and so lacking a human-type rational saveable soul.[28] There have been dissenting voices in the Christian mainstream (including Bishop Kallistos himself). Even those who, like modern Jehovah's Witnesses, say (and I quote) 'Do animals have souls? No'[29] often soften the blow by saying (dissonantly with their view of the soul, perhaps) that animals might play a part in the renewed creation which will arise in the Messianic Age, realizing the vision of Isaiah's holy mountain, where the wolf will lie down with the lamb,[30] and where, presumably, even cats will be placidly vegetarian.

The view that animals will be shut out of the afterlife is psychologically unsustainable for most of us. Heaven wouldn't be heaven without animals. Martin Luther, when asked by his children if their favourite animals would accompany them to eternity, is said to have replied: 'If, when you get to heaven, you want your dog there, it will be there.' He continued, however, questioning whether, given all the other glories of heaven, we will actually want our dogs there. To that, many an earnest and pious dog owner would give a resounding 'yes!', arguing that they are so enmeshed with their pets that not only would happiness be inconceivable without them, but that if the pet is excised, there wouldn't be much of the owner left to save. Luther himself, as his own dog was dying, said to it: 'Be thou comforted, little dog; thou too in Resurrection shall have a little golden tail.'

Theology tends to follow psychology – even in the ancient citadels of Christianity. C.S. Lewis, a great animal lover, contended that an animal that is attached in life to a human might be saved by being caught up with the saved soul of its master or mistress.[31] That seems rather hard on unloved animals, and connotes a low view of the wild. It saves lapdogs, but damns squirrels.

Pope Francis may have settled the matter for Catholics – and settled it in favour of animal salvation. In the encyclical *Laudato Si* he wrote that 'Eternal life will be a shared experience of awe, in which each creature, resplendently transfigured, will take its rightful place and have something to give those poor men and women who will have been liberated once and for all…'[32] The import of these words is much discussed, but 'each creature' would seem to include non-human animals. If so dead pets, continue (but more gloriously) the work of pet-hood they began here.

Whatever the ecclesiastical authorities say, many modern pet owners find it impossible to believe that something as solid and alive as their pet can be annihilated by something as trivial as bodily death. Souls seem to be so much more robust than bodies.

The playwright Eugene O'Neill had a Dalmatian called Blemie. When Blemie died, he (Blemie) left behind a last will and testament, which was published in 1940. 'I have little in the way of material things to leave', it said.

> Dogs are wiser than men. They do not set great store upon things. They do not waste their days hoarding property. They do not ruin their sleep worrying about how to keep the objects they have, and to obtain the objects they have not. There is nothing of value I

> have to bequeath except my love and my faith. These I leave to all those who have loved me…

Blemie asked to be remembered, but not to be mourned for too long. It would be a sorrow to leave those he had loved, 'he' said, 'but not a sorrow to die. Dogs do not fear death as men do. We accept it as part of life, not as something alien and terrible which destroys life.' He went onto to speculate about what may come after. He wanted to believe that

> there is a Paradise where one is always young and full-bladdered; where all the day one dillies and dallies with an amorous multitude of houris [lovely nymphs], beautifully spotted; where jack rabbits that run fast but not too fast (like the houris) are as the sands of the desert; where each blissful hour is mealtime; where in long evenings there are a million fireplaces with logs forever burning, and one curls oneself up and blinks into the flames and nods and dreams, remembering the old brave days on earth, and the love of one's Master and Mistress. I am afraid this is too much for even such a dog as I am to expect. But peace, at least, is certain. Peace and long rest for weary old heart and head and limbs, and eternal sleep in the earth I have loved so well.

He signed off by begging his owners to get another dog:

> I have never had a narrow, jealous spirit. I have always held that most dogs are good (and one cat, the black one I have permitted to share the living room rug during the evenings, whose affection I have tolerated in a kindly spirit, and in rare sentimental moods, even reciprocated a trifle). Some dogs, of course, are better than others. Dalmatians, naturally, as everyone knows, are best. So I suggest a Dalmatian as my successor.… To him I bequeath my collar and leash and my overcoat and raincoat, made to order in 1929 at Hermes in Paris.… I am sure he will do his utmost not to appear a mere gauche provincial dog.

And a last word:

> Whenever you visit my grave, say to yourselves with regret but also with happiness in your hearts at the remembrance of my long happy life with you: 'Here lies one who loved us and whom we loved'. No matter how deep my sleep I shall hear you, and not all the power of death can keep my spirit from wagging a grateful tail.[33]

It is not a joke. It is a serious and plangent attempt to reconcile despair and hope: to make meaning of an animal's life and the human life it has shaped. Blemie was not sure that there was a heaven for dogs, but he devoutly hoped there was, and for him it would have to be a full-bladdered, brimming-bowled version of this world – a place where the important relationships in this life were maintained and enhanced.

We see the same devout hope – but also a good deal of conviction – on any website dealing with pet death.

In Chapter 7 we visited the site of Vets2 Home: Peaceful Pet Goodbyes – the vets specializing in at-home euthanasia. It has its own virtual memorial wall, where owners post tributes. Many owners believe that they will see their pets again. There is, for instance, a video celebrating the life of 'Woolly Harper', a dog 'who was drifted off by Dr Suzen', age 15. There you can watch Woolly gambolling on the beach and swimming in the river, to the musical backdrop of a song which declares 'Goodbye friend, until the next time.... See you somewhere, sometime along the road.'[34] 'Until we meet again', writes Melissa, of her, cat, George. Julia and Neal were confident about the fate of their dog Poppy, and she was constantly present to them: 'We know we will meet her again somewhere in the cosmos, for now I will feel her energy in the rain, her warmth of character in the sun, her playfulness in the wind.' 'God you take care of my precious lady Princess Bacon cat. I'll meet you at the Rainbow Bridge in time', wrote Abi C. Dee and Rick were 'sure Barney is still running free on the beach', and Christina and

Rachel Godfrey, similarly, imagined that their cat Oscar was 'no doubt running around whilst in the sun, attempting to catch butterflies once again'. 'See you in Heaven baby bear our special Beadle', was part of the epitaph of Cleo, a cat, and the owners' 'beautiful fur baby'. Lady Catherine Blitz was very theologically explicit: 'My Darling Pug Yumi has flown up to Rainbow Bridge', she wrote.

> God had called home my beloved loved one. You were always there to love and comfort me with an undying love no human can give. You came to me in my time [of] great need, it was then I realized God had sent me a little Earth Angel in my time of need. I loved you with all my heart, and will always love you, you are still in my heart and at my side.... You are now with God in Heaven you can run and play pain free. One day we [will] re-unite in Heaven so we can run together.[35]

Of the 111 memorials on the site, 32 make some explicit reference to the pet's afterlife – not including references such as 'rest easy', 'sleep tight', 'lives in my heart', 'I always say goodnight to her ashes', 'sleep peacefully now ... next to the pond where you liked to go for a drink'.

This is a snapshot – not a scientific survey. The numbers are small, and there may be various confounding biases. The site, for instance, represents only owners who have asked for their animals to be put to sleep. Guilt may have nudged some owners to suppose an afterlife in which they can make reparation. But I suspect any error is in the opposite direction. Many of the memorials are terse and contain no detailed reflection of any kind. There may, too, be some embarrassment about making a public declaration of one's theological convictions. In any event, 32/111 (nearly 29 per cent) is a substantial proportion.

This same conclusion has been intriguingly demonstrated by a survey of over a thousand inscriptions in four British pet cemeteries, representing burials from the late nineteenth to the early twentieth century: England's first public pet cemetery at Hyde Park, London; a suburban burial ground in Ilford, Essex; and Jesmond Dene and Northumberland Park in the north-east of England. In Victorian England, theological strictures made it hard for bereaved owners to talk explicitly about an afterlife for their pets, and generally, with a few poignant exceptions, they did not. The authors of the study give, as an example of an exception, the inscription on the grave of 'Grit' (died 1900), in Hyde Park: 'Could I think we'd meet again, it would lighten half my pain.' You can feel the caution. The owner was hedging their bets about whether there was in fact a pet heaven. It was a declaration that would get past the most conservative vicar.

By the mid-twentieth century things were different. The church either did not matter so much to the bereaved owners or had softened its own stance. Not only were there more references to the afterlife, but the references there were more confident. Hope was beginning to turn to *expectation*.[36]

That expectation seems now to be even more common. While many say that we are becoming more secular, our attitude, at least in relation to our pets, has become more (or at least more overtly) religious. The evidence is hard to gather and interpret, but our pets may be *making* us more religious.

Pets seem to be effective evangelists. Thomas Hardy, a notorious atheist, had this to say in his poem 'Dead "Wessex", the Dog to the Household'.

> You may hear a jump or trot,
> Wistful ones,
> You may hear a jump or trot –
> Mine, as 'twere –
> You may hear a jump or trot
> On the stair or path or plot;
> But I shall cause it not,
> Be not there.

Should you call as when I knew you,
Wistful ones,
Should you call as when I knew you,
Shared your home;
Should you call as when I knew you,
I shall not turn to view you,
I shall not listen to you,
Shall not come.

It is notionally a nihilistic poem, of a piece with most of Hardy's desolate corpus. But am I alone in thinking that Hardy protests a little too much? That Wessex, even if he will not turn, listen or come, is still there, somewhere; disobedient rather than non-existent?

★

One final and hubristic enquiry: might the relationship indeed survive physical death? There are many reports, from many countries and many ages, of animal ghosts.[37] A few examples will suffice.

Littlecote House, in Hungerford, Berkshire, is a famously haunted place. One of its many ghosts, seen by several staff members, is said to be a black dog. It looks solid, but if anyone tries to stroke it, their hand goes straight through.

Another ghostly black dog – a curly-coated retriever – haunts Leeds Castle in Kent, passes through walls and closed doors, and is sometimes a harbinger of misfortune.

A large, headless tabby cat caused mayhem in a Manchester house, screeching, growling and snarling, staring with big red eyes, and jumping onto the human inhabitants of the house.[38]

And finally a report from Ontario, Canada:

> I was on my way home. I was walking down a road where there were no streetlights, when I saw this big white dog come across the road. It was jumping as it moved in slow motion and just went right through the fence on the other side, and on up through the field. I watched as it ran, still in slow motion, until I lost sight of it.[39]

One psychic maintains that there is an important distinction between human and animal ghosts. I quote the (unnamed) author at length, not contending that they know the truth about hauntings, but because the piece summarizes many of the intuitions about the human–animal bond we have seen in other contexts:

> Most hauntings center around a trauma – a tragedy or sudden death creates an emotional 'bruise' that traps spirits in time and space. That's why battlefields and historically violent places, such as the Tower of London, are frequently the sites of paranormal activity. Animal ghosts, on the other hand, are less likely to be the result of agony or hurt in life.
>
> The majority of household animal ghosts stick around for more benevolent reasons. Their attachment isn't about past trauma, but a vibrant emotional connection with their owners or their homes. The connection between master and pet can be so powerful in life that it borders on telepathy. After death, that spiritual attachment does not fade. That's why the ghost of a pet may act as a guardian angel, a divine protector. For example, animals that are loyal and defensive in life, like Rottweilers, might not see death as a sufficient reason to leave their post. There are stories in the psychic community of phantom barks scaring away would-be home intruders; most likely these cries are the defenses of an old pet.
>
> Of course, animal guardian angels don't always wait to spring into action until the danger is near. Much as in life, they can ease the burden of an emotional struggle with kisses and cuddles. The question is whether an animal ghost's owner can consciously perceive its affection. Not everyone is well-attuned to psychic phenomena, so not everyone can experience the presence of an animal ghost.[40]

We are together with our pets in life – so closely together that there is only a fuzzy border between the pet and the owner. And together, or, so many believe, in death – when perhaps the border is even fuzzier, and perhaps dissolves altogether.

★

Some devoted pet owners do not believe in the prospect of meeting their beloved animal after its death, or cannot wait that long. If they are rich, they may seek technological resurrection. It is called cloning.

ViaGen Pets of Cedar Park, Texas, will, on receipt of a tissue sample and $50,000, clone your dog or cat. 'Lasting Love' is one of their bylines, and Barbra Streisand – who used ViaGen to make two clones (Miss Violet and Miss Scarlett) of her dog, Coton de Tulear Samantha, deceased – their most famous client.[41]

When a client's cat, Ceaser (*sic*) died, his owner was inconsolable. 'I have a very rich life filled with many friends but Ceaser was something else entirely. From 18 to 33 I truly had a best friend, no matter the day, I always had him to bring a smile. The complete unwavering love and companionship is only second to my wife.' So Ceaser's cells were extracted and sent off to ViaGen. At the time of the testimonial the cloning process was not complete, but, said the owner, 'I know my child will be reborn.... What's a splurge on luxury items when you can bring back a piece of your heart that you thought was broken forever.'[42]

The owner of a small, crooked-faced cat called Doodle had decided to clone the cat while he (Doodle) was still alive, so that Doodle could meet a cloned version of himself. Sadly Doodle died before he could meet his twin, but the cloning went ahead. It was a great success.

> Exactly 1 year after I started the cloning process, I received Rumbler, Doodle's clone. He is almost exactly like Doodle. He has the same crooked face mask and the same wonderful smile. He has mostly the same personality, even down to the littlest quirks. The biggest difference: It seems like Rumbler is just a little friendlier than Doodle, probably due to his upbringing. He is the light of my life. He sleeps with me every night. All of my other cats love him just as much as I do. I can't wait to wake up every morning to see what day we will have together!...

> Rumbler couldn't be more Doodle-y. It feels like Doodle is inside Rumbler so I don't have to miss him as much anymore. The first day I got him he knew his name and he came when I snapped my fingers. This is just one example of many little things that are so strange for him to know as a kitten so soon after his arrival. I know this won't be everybody's experience, but for the rest of my life I want to have a Doodle clone by my side....
>
> Having Rumbler is like getting the chance to spend another lifetime with my Doodle boy.[43]

These are heart-warming stories, whatever the ethical objections.[44] But however happy the owners might be, their $50,000 has not triumphed over the grave. Ceaser will never again bring a smile to his owner's face. Doodle is not Rumbler. Cats, dogs, we, and all creatures, are very much more than our genes, and to confuse a creature which possesses some of Doodle's characteristics with Doodle himself is to do Doodle an injustice: to imply that he was simply a collection of attributes. It is a denial of the quintessential, indefinable, downright mystical Doodle-ness that made Doodle lovable. Genetic reductionism is passé in the academy, but still alive and well in the marketplace, as Doodle and Ceaser are not. Only a cell nucleus of the dead pet is used for cloning: there is cytoplasmic DNA and RNA too, whose contribution is mysterious but real. In any event, what seems to matter most is not what genes you have, but which are switched on, and to what extent. The environment plays an increasingly recognized part in the switching.

The confusion of substance and attributes is even more dramatically on display in a resurrection option for the (relatively) indigent. For £356, Cuddle Clone will create a bespoke cuddly model of your dead pet.

'I lost my best friend, side kick, soul mate – my everything, Layla two weeks ago', wrote one satisfied client, and 'decided to rush-order a Cuddle Clone.... When I saw the postal service pull up my heart started racing. Upon opening the package I could not contain my emotions. Wow. I thought I would be so sad, yet the second I picked her up I was so comforted and cried in a joyful way.'

'I chose the option to have a zipper pouch installed [in the Cuddle Clone of her pet, Oliver]', wrote another, 'and I'm so glad I did. I was able to put my boy's ashes in there, and holding his plush replica is so much more comforting than holding a box...'

And finally,

> [having] put our beloved Zander down last month ... having this Cuddle Clone has helped us to transition from an empty house, to one that still shares his memory. Our 14 month old crawls to it constantly, and snuggles him, and our 4 year old brings him to the couch to watch shows together like our real Zander use[d] to do. It's helping us to grieve in our own small, slow way. We weren't ready to say goodbye, so this helps heal a huge wound that is just now starting to feel less tender.[45]

Is actual genetic cloning, or 'Cuddle Cloning', really any different from having your dead mother's photo on the wall, or her ashes on the mantlepiece, or feeling close to your dead father because you're wearing his suit? Would we want a clone of a dead brother living in the spare room, or to watch movies alongside a realistic doll made in the image of a favourite dead nephew?

I cannot speak for everyone, but I suspect there is a consensus that the ViaGen and Cuddle Clone enterprises are somehow – perhaps obscurely, but undoubtedly – different from the photo, the ashes or the suit, and that our intuitions tend to protest against human clones or dolls in a way that they do not against Rumbler or the fabric version of Zander.

So, nearing the end of this book – a book which may often seem to have minimized the difference between humans and pets – we see a quiet but insistent belief, after all, in human specialness.

What are we, that we think ourselves different from dogs, cats and horses? What are we, that we think ourselves tied to them? Or part of them? What are we, who can see ourselves most clearly when a hamster holds up the mirror? What are we, who are lonely in the company of our own species? What are we, the great manipulators of our environment, who cannot manipulate ourself out of dependence upon creatures we often call 'lower', but often treat as gods?

NINE

People and their pets; pets and their people

Early on a Friday morning I fought my way through the belching Cairo traffic to a road running below the Moqattam Hills along one edge of the gigantic necropolis known as the City of the Dead, where many of Egypt's poorest live amongst the tombs. For half a day, for half a mile, the road is the site of one of the largest live animal markets in Africa.

You can find just about anything there. When we first walked up the road at seven o'clock an emu was in leg irons. When we came back at ten it was strung up, skinned and disembowelled, its trachea hanging down like a vacuum-cleaner hose.

Snakes, rearing up and thrashing in the mounting heat, banged their noses on the glass of their tanks; bats hung like battered shoes from their cages; shit-stained barn owls sat hunched with tight-shut eyes, ignoring the dead rats from the next stall slung to them for food. Little parakeets were the colour of the dust kicked up from the road. A lizard was eating its brother's tail, but the brother didn't seem to care. A one-eyed eagle slumped on the handlebars of a bicycle was the only bird of the tens of thousands in the half-mile that had room to spread its wings. But it couldn't, because both its wings were broken.

It was the foxes that got to me. Hundreds of them, mostly red foxes, of the sort we know in Europe, but smaller. Many of them were just cubs.

'I can't bear their despair', said the friend who had taken me there. But it was their hope that was intolerable. They were too weak and tired to snap at the flies that lapped at their sores, but their ears swivelled round, hoping for the squeak of an opening cage door, and they always had an eye open, wondering if the next set of passing legs would help them go back to the wild world.

There was great pain there, and great cruelty and callousness.

The market was packed. We had to elbow our way through the crowd.

The attraction for the crowd was not the sight of suffering. The people were not perverts, and anyway there is quite enough lurid suffering on Cairo's streets if you like that kind of thing. They were curious people who watched and wondered. Many had come a long way to watch.

They had not come only to watch, but to buy – and buy with money they could not spare.

A man bought one of the little foxes. He was obviously poor. He bargained hard for it, but the price must have hurt. He picked it up by the scruff, pushed it into a homemade wooden box, and took it away. I imagine it died of grief or diarrhoea within the week.

Why did he want it? I think he wanted to feel the eyes of a predator on him, as his Pleistocene ancestors did as they sat round the formative campfire. He wanted to know that he had some advantage over the predator, or some kind of solidarity with it. He wanted to get back to where we have all come from. He wanted his teetering tenement to be part of the desert beyond the hills.

*

Here is Laura Hobgood-Oster seeking to summarize the relationship between humans and their pet dogs:

> one of the most significant aspects of dogs related to human cultural ideas is that they exist somewhere in the betwixt and between, in the threshold. Not fully animal, but not fully human, they both bridge the gap and exist within it. They connect humans to nature while simultaneously providing a border between humans and nature.[1]

That's one way of putting part of the answer, but it is too neat to do justice to creatures as complex as dogs or humans, let alone to the relationship between two such complex entities.

We say that we love our pets. We call them our children, our fur babies, our confidants and our best friends. They sleep in our beds, we drape them with bling, work like mad to pay for their maintenance, and give them an annual allowance that would save the lives of many sub-Saharan children. They consume much of our time. We pick up their faeces (and often, bafflingly, hang the bags on trees), endure their bad breath, and scratch ourselves raw when their fleas bite us. We like to have them beside us as we work, and some of us say that we cannot work without them. We often think that they understand us better than our human friends and partners, despite, or more likely because, we do not speak with them in the human language that so often falls short, and misrepresents. They remind us of our pre-linguistic childhoods, when the world was more fascinating and simpler. Their eyes are at the level of our eyes when we crawled around as babies. They feel the ground with all four feet, as we once did, and use their noses, as we once did, and enjoy rolling in the mud, as we once did. They taste reality as it is, as we once could, and they teach us how to do it again. We walk boldly into dark caves if they are beside us. They help us talk to strangers, and bite the strangers who try to hurt us.

We define our home as the place where the pets are. When they die we are devastated, and the house is no longer a home. We look forward to meeting them again over the other side of the rainbow bridge, if that's our metaphysical inclination, tweak our theology so that they are saved, hear their ghosts padding alongside us on our walks, write more gushing memorial poems about them than we do about our parents, weep at their graves, wear their ashes over our hearts, zip the ashes into tailor-made compartments sewn into huggable models of the dead animal, or, if we're rich, squirt their nuclei into denucleated egg cells which we then incubate in the uterus of a surrogate bitch to create a twin. We have dogs rather than children.

We love them, we say, for themselves, yet we surgically remove their testicles, wombs and ovaries, trim their ears and tails, and breed them so that their brains and noses are squashed, their skin folded and an oasis of infection, and their legs twisted. We lock them up all day in the boxes we call our apartments, ensure that they never see a rabbit, and drag them away from enthralling smells at the foot of lampposts. We keep them in centrally heated rooms when they would be happier in a kennel outside. If, when we're driving, a child and a cat are both in the road, and we have to choose between the cat and the child, we unhesitatingly kill the cat – and quite right too.

We say – as I have done – that they connect us to the wild, but we think that one cat's life is more valuable than the cumulative lives of the hundreds of wild birds and small mammals it kills in a year, keep the cat going by pumping it full of medicines made on an industrial estate in Switzerland, and feed it on sterilized paste made from the lungs of factory-farmed pigs. To get rid of our dog's parasites we use compounds which wipe out the invertebrate infrastructure of our rivers. We take our dogs to romp through colonies of ground-nesting birds. We deploy wild things as the emblems and weapons of unnatural organizations such as nation states.

It is all very complex, contradictory and downright strange. Much of the strangeness is exhilarating and should be celebrated. But there is an ugly dissonance within the strangeness – a dissonance that sounds like hypocrisy or, at best, like the distinctive clang of unexamined presumptions smashing against one another.

The dissonance occurs because of what we've become since the last Ice Age.

★

One indicator of what we've become is that we increasingly give our pets the names we used to give only to our children.

This is a very recent phenomenon – perhaps just thirty or so years old.[2] Until then, Child Sarah was Child Sarah, and Cat Fluffy was Cat Fluffy. Names, as we saw at the start of this book and at the start of the Judaeo-Christian story of the created order, matter: they are not just labels, but make a statement about the nature of the named thing, and about the authority of whoever it is who does the naming.

To give humans the same name as our animals denotes a confusion of categories – a confounding of identities. It dilutes our dignity and that of our animals, for dignity involves being oneself as opposed to someone or something else. To call the cat 'Sarah' marks a radical shift in our self-understanding, or perhaps a shift from self-understanding to self non-understanding.

We have seen repeatedly throughout this book that our pets show us what we are. What they show us most clearly is that we no longer know what we are, and that this is a very recent and accelerating phenomenon. The grating weirdnesses we have met on our journey are often symptoms of a debilitating malady.

There may be something even more sinister going on. Collis Harvey points to a growing trend not just to use children's names for pets, but to use pet names for children. Trixi gambols through the classroom. Bambi grazes in the school canteen. 'It is as if the animals and children are swapping places.'[3] In numbers, at any rate, children and pets are indeed swapping places. We saw in Chapter 4 that the human birth rate in the west is plummeting, while pet numbers are growing.

We're increasingly unapologetic about the exchange or conflation of roles and status. We've seen how we drape animals in bling, feed them the organic, free-range food we'd like to have ourselves, call them our babies and imagine that they will share our eternal future. And now we expressly assume that they share not just our beds and our leisure activities but our tastes. 'Taste-tested by humans: Made for dogs', announces an advert for dog food.[4] It's a declaration not just of companionship or solidarity or friendship, but of something tantamount to *identity*.

'I love not Man the less, but Nature more', announced Byron.[5] That's not such an unhealthy state of affairs, but it might not explain modern attitudes towards humans and animals. We may be coming to see our capacity for love as finite – like a pizza: that slice for animals, that slice for music, that slice for ecology. Sorry, there's none left for humans.[6] We might be starting to love Man less, and animals, if not actually to blame, might at least be the beneficiaries of love diverted damagingly away from humans. Gavin Steingo talks about a 'new misanthropy', producing slogans such as 'Dogs: Because people suck'.[7] 'Dogs make me happy. You not so much' announces a very popular tee-shirt.

What should we make of this? Many things, but mainly this. We're confused. We no longer know what we are, and therefore how to act. To love a cat more than we love our parents or our putative children or our neighbour shows that we've lost our way. Pets are ethical litmus: they show us that we've gone wrong, and how we've gone wrong. They help us to diagnose our condition. That's useful, for you can't have therapy without diagnosis.

One final observation: one that hints at an effective treatment for this modern crisis. It is simply that pet ownership is not just a response to our own domestication. John Bradshaw has demonstrated that hunter–gatherer communities are enthusiastic pet keepers, keeping many species, including dogs, bears, wolves, raccoons, tapirs, agouti, coati, monkeys, ocelots, sloths, hyenas, flying foxes, sun bears, gibbons and many bird species. In fact, says Bradshaw, fish are the only class of pets almost wholly absent from traditional societies.[8]

Keeping these wild pets often demands substantial investment. Young animals – typically the offspring of adults killed by hunters – are often breastfed by the women: Māori women are wet nurses to puppies and piglets; women in New Guinea to piglets; the women of Ainu, in Japan, to bears; and indigenous Australian women to dingoes.

In 1950 Gavin Maxwell walked down a steep hill in the Northwest Highlands of Scotland to a remote seashore cottage lent to him by a friend. It was as remote as it is possible to get in Britain. There was no electricity and no telephone. He built furniture from driftwood. The nearest village was an arduous walk and then a drive, or a trip by boat on the capricious sea.

The cottage became famous as 'Camusfeàrna' in the *Ring of Bright Water* trilogy.[9] Maxwell had a dog – a Springer Spaniel called Jonnie – but Jonnie was not enough. Nor were the deer, the dolphins in the loch, or the eagles over the mountain. Maxwell fell in love with a succession of otters which shared his bed and changed his life. They were tame-ish for Maxwell, and generally for the keepers who helped out, but they remained wild at heart – as Terry Nutkins, one of the keepers, found when 'his' otter, Edal, turned on him and chewed him. Two fingers had to be amputated.

Maxwell lived in the wild and acknowledged his dependence on it, yet wanted *more* of it. It is the same for the pet-keeping hunter-gatherers. The wild isn't wild enough. For them, so for us: it is not enough to live in the wild; the wild has to live in us – in our houses, chairs and beds.

Proper pet ownership – ownership the way the hunter–gatherers do it, and unlike the way we have recently tended to do it – is the ownership of proper animals: animals, that is, that are still themselves, with normal psyches, physiologies and organs. Ownership of this kind is not ownership at all, for nothing can own something that is truly itself. Only if the animal is still itself – still wild – will it do the job we ask of it: to be a piece of companionable wildness in the house, reminding us of what we are. The Egyptian bought the fox to do this job. That's why the cat is lying on your lap.

We are still, constitutionally, hunter–gatherers. That's why we, too, want wild things on the sofa, whatever the cost in time, money or inconvenience. It takes much longer than 30 or 300 or 3,000 years to breed or pummel the Pleistocene out of us. But we've gone wrong in various remediable ways. Our pets can help to restore us to our factory settings.

We're used to saying that dog owners are like their dogs. But we're all more like newts. We are amphibians, flopping between the wild and the tame, but more at home in the wild. We feel ill at ease in the homes we've made. We feel we've sold out.

We use animals – the wolves at our hearths, the tigers curled up on the chair, the foxes dying in cages in our apartments – to tell us that we are really in the wild when we're at home.[10]

This is a big job. It is hard to be a pet. No wonder we're confused about what they really are.

Notes

PREFACE

1. Katherine Grier, *Pets in America: A History*, University of North Carolina Press, Chapel Hill NC, 2006, p. 6.

THE WEIRDNESS OF PETS

1. 2024 figures, from UK pet food industry statistics.
2. Estimates provided by Honey's: https://honeysrealdogfood.com; accessed 27 January 2025. The cooked and raw recipes are based on beef, pork, chicken, turkey and venison. The estimates allow 5 hours' labour for the cooked food, and 4 hours for the raw. The relatively greater cost per kg of dog weight for smaller dogs is due to smaller dogs having, generally, a higher metabolic rate.
3. Office for National Statistics, as analysed in www.nimblefins.co.uk; accessed 27 January 2025.
4. According to the Royal Society for the Protection of Birds, 2024. The average pet cat brings home five kills a year. Probably most of the bird kills are by stray and feral cats.
5. www.who.int/news-room/fact-sheets/detail/rabies; https://pmc.ncbi.nlm.nih.gov/articles/PMC3484763; both accessed 27 January 2025.

HOW THE ANIMALS GOT INTO OUR HOMES

1. Genesis 1: 31.
2. Genesis 2: 19–20.
3. Genesis 2: 20–22.
4. Genesis 3: 19.
5. Numbers 22: 21–38.
6. Qur'an 27:16.
7. Bava Kamma 83a; *Shulchan Aruch Harav*, Shemirat Haguf Vehanefesh 3.
8. Leviticus 22: 24.
9. www.chabad.org/library/article_cdo/aid/5291109/jewish/Judaism-and-Pet-Ownership-18–FAQs.htm; accessed 27 January 2025.
10. Muhammad Al-Bukhari 3225; Muslim ibn al-Hajjaj 2106.
11. Niko Kontovas, personal communication, 2025.

12. Muhammad Al-Bukhari 6203; Muslim ibn al-Hajjaj 2150.
13. Al-Hafiz Ibn Hajar, *Fath al-Bari* 10/584.
14. *What a Fish Knows: The Inner Lives of Our Underwater Cousins*, Scientific American Press, New York, 2017.
15. See S. Jeannin, C. Gilbert, M. Amy and G. Leboucher, 'Pet-directed speech draws adult dogs' attention more efficiently than adult-directed speech', *Nature: Scientific Reports*, 7(1), 2017, p. 4980.
16. See www.apa.org/news/press/releases/2009/08/dogs-think; accessed 27 January 2025.
17. M. Ohta, Y. Sakuma, T. Onaka, K. Mogi and T. Kikusui, 'Oxytocin-gaze positive loop and the coevolution of human–dog bonds', *Science*, 348(6232), 2015, pp. 333–6; see the discussion in J. Howard, *Wonderdog: How the Science of Dogs Changed the Science of Life*, Bloomsbury Sigma, London, 2022, pp. 222–39. T. Romero, M. Nagasawa, K. Mogi, T. Hasegawa and T. Kikusui, 'Oxytocin promotes social bonding in dogs', *Proceedings of the National Academy of Sciences*, 111(25), 2014, pp. 9085–90; K. Murata, M. Nagasawa, T. Onaka, N. Kanemaki, S. Nakamura, K. Tsubota and T. Kikusui, 'Increase of tear volume in dogs after reunion with owners is mediated by oxytocin', *Current Biology*, 32(16), 2022, pp. R869–R870.
18. For discussion, see Jacky Colliss Harvey, *The Animal's Companion: People and Their Pets: A 26,000 Year-Old Love Story,* Allen & Unwin, London, 2019, p. 30.
19. For discussion, see Howard, *Wonderdog*, p. 43.
20. There is a debate about whether, at least in humans, smaller brains mean cognitive decline. It has been suggested that smaller brains might mean that the remaining neurones are closer to one another, facilitating neuronal connectivity.
21. John Bradshaw, *The Animals Among Us: The New Science of Anthrozoology,* Allen Lane, London, 2017, p. 286.
22. Laura Hobgood-Oster, *A Dog's History of the World: Canines and the Domestication of Humans*, Baylor University Press, Waco TX, p. 129.
23. Carlos Driscoll, Juliet Clutton Brock, Andrew Kitchener and Stephen O'Brien, 'The evolution of house cats', *Scientific American*, 1 June 2009.
24. S. Doherty, M. Krajcarz, A. Carmagnini, E. Dimopoulos, A. Jamieson, J.M. Alves and N. Sykes, 'Redefining the timing and circumstances of cat domestication, their dispersal trajectories, and the extirpation of European wildcats' bioRxiv, March 2025.
25. One indication of the scale of the industry is the discovery by an Egyptian peasant in 1888, at Beni Hasan, about 100 miles south of Cairo, of a mass grave containing cat mummies. 180,000 of them were exported to England, and used as fertilizer. Huge numbers have been found too at Saqqara. R. Ciliberti, A. Tosi and M. Licata, 'Feline mummies as a fertilizer. Criticisms on the destruction of archaeozoological remains during the 19th century', *Archaeofauna*, 29, 2020, pp. 129–35.
26. Herodotus, *Histories*, Book 2, Chapter 66.
27. The spread in other directions may involve rather different stories. Take China, for example. From around 5,400 years ago, leopard cats were in some sort of commensal relationship with humans. Their alliance seems to have diminished from around 1,800 years ago – probably as a result of dynastic and associated socioeconomic changes. Domestic cats were very late arrivals in China – long after the other main domestic animals such as cattle, sheep, goats and horses. They probably came along the Silk Road, perhaps as the companions of traders, or as rodent-killers, or as commodities. The first unequivocally identified domestic cat in China was found in Tongwan City in Shaanti, western China. Its remains have been carbon-dated to *c.* 1,200 years ago. It was white or white-spotted, short-haired and long-tailed.
28. There has been a recent and intriguing suggestion that cats may sometimes covertly, and at a distance, shadow dogs when the dogs are taken out for a walk.

29. For further discussion, see A. Hulme-Beaman, D. Orton and T. Cucchi, 'The origins of the domesticate brown rat (*Rattus norvegicus*) and its pathways to domestication', *Anim Front*, 11(3), 19 June 2021, pp. 78–86.
30. Edward H. Schafer, 'Falconry in T'ang times', *T'oung Pao* 46, 1959, pp. 293–338.
31. Mahmood Kolnegari et al., 'Falconry petroglyphs in Iran: new findings on the nexus between ancient humans and birds of prey', *European Journal of Wildlife Research*, 67(3), 2021, p. 38.
32. J.V. Canby, 'Falconry (hawking) in Hittite lands', *Journal of Near Eastern Studies*, 61(3), July 2002, pp. 161–201.
33. Hans J. Epstein, 'The origin and earliest history of falconry', *Isis* 34(6), 1943, pp. 497–509. http://www.jstor.org/stable/225894.
34. Book 10, trans. H. Rackham, Loeb Classical Library 330, Harvard University Press, Cambridge MA, 1938.
35. Percy Bysshe Shelley, *Letters: Shelley in Italy*, Clarendon Press, Oxford, 1964, p. 330.
36. Cited in Colliss Harvey, *The Animal's Companion*. The dog died from the toxic dye.
37. Bodleian: Uncatalogued JJC. Pet related items.
38. Julie Hecht and Alexandria Horowitz, 'Seeing dogs: human preferences for dog physical attributes', *Anthrozoos* 28, 2015, pp. 153–63. See too S. Nakajima, M. Yamamoto and N. Yoshimoto,'Dogs look like their owners: replications with racially homogenous owner portraits', *Anthrozoös*, 22(2), 2009, pp. 173–81 – which shows that we think that dogs look their owners.
39. Katrina E. Holland, 'Acquiring a pet dog: a review of factors affecting the decision-making of prospective dog owners', *Animals* 9(4), 2019, p. 124.
40. Holland (ibid.) comments: 'a more nuanced understanding of the importance that adopters of non-purebreds report to confer on appearance when choosing their dog would be worthy of future study, to investigate why owner–dog resemblance does not appear to exist in these circumstances.'
41. C. Payne and K. Jaffe, 'Self seeks like: many humans choose their dog pets following rules used for assortative mating', *J Ethol* 23, 2005, pp. 15–18.
42. Holland ('Acquiring a pet dog') notes, however, that '[t]he level at which the resemblance between owner and dog exists is not explained by these studies. Whether the resemblance exists at the level of physical attributes, such as size, or at a stylistic level, such as a friendly appearance, could be profitably further explored in future studies.'
43. G. Tesfom and N.J. Birch, 'Does definition of self predict adopter dog breed choice?', *Int Rev Public Nonprofit Mark* 10, 2013, pp. 103–27.
44. Vets in the UK reported 1 in 14 dogs as overweight – almost certainly a significant underestimate, since probably relatively few owners seek veterinary help for obesity: see Pegram et al., 'Frequency, breed disposition and demographic risk factors for overweight status in dogs in the UK', *Journal of Small Animal Practice*, 62(7), 2021.

CHILDHOOD AND ADOLESCENCE

1. Cited in Colliss Harvey, *The Animal's Companion*, p. 5.
2. Genesis 3:7.
3. Colliss Harvey, *The Animal's Companion*, pp. 4–5.
4. *Summa Theologica*, Pars II 2a 2ae, quaest. XXV. Art III, Turin, 1922, vol. 3, pp. 149–55.
5. London, British Library, MS. Cotton Cleopatra D viii fol 109r–v.
6. Lydia H. Sigourney, *Letters to Mothers*, Harper & Brothers, New York, 1838, pp. 35–6. See too the discussion in Grier, *Pets in America*, pp. 27–8.
7. 'Dogs and Cats', in *Stories and Sketches for the Young, The Writings of Harriet Beecher Stowe,* vol. 14, Riverside edn [1896], AMS Press, New York, 1967, p. 109.

8. Genesis 3:1, Orthodox Study Bible, Thomas Nelson, Nashville, 2008.
9. Genesis 3:14, Orthodox Study Bible.
10. See, for instance, an 1848 children's book, *The Dog, as an Example of Fidelity*, published by the General Protestant Episcopal Sunday School Union.
11. 'Baby's visits to Chester': Bodleian Library, MS. Eng. Lett. d. 288.
12. M. Minatoya, A. Ikeda-Araki, C. Miyashita, S. Itoh, S. Kobayashi, K. Yamazaki, Y. Ait Bamai, Y. Saijo, Y. Sato, Y. Ito Y and R. Kishi, the Japan Environment and Children's Study Group, 'Asssociation between early life child development and family dog ownership: a prospective birth cohort study of the Japan environment and children's study', *Int J Environ Res Public Health*, 18(13), 2 July 2021, p. 7082. The same study went on to say that 'Further, a number of studies have suggested that family dog ownership is associated with better health outcomes. For instance, family dog ownership is associated with walking and physical activity in school children.... living with dogs during early infancy may decrease the risk of developmental delay in the communication, gross motor, problem-solving, and personal-social domains.'
13. Sarah Josepha Hale, *Poems for Our Children: Designed for Families, Sabbath Schools and Infant Schools, Written to Inculcate Moral Truths and Virtuous Sentiments*, Marsh, Capen & Lyon, Boston MA, 1830; and *The Juvenile Miscellany*, Putnam & Hunt, Boston MA, 1826–36.
14. Troy, New York, 1840, discussed in Grier, *Pets in America,* p. 146.
15. Roberts Brothers, published in two volumes, 1868 and 1869.
16. *The Frugal Housewife: Dedicated to Those Who Are Not Ashamed of Economy*, Marsh & Capen, and Carter & Hendee, Boston MA, 1829.
17. Richard Bentley, London, 1844.
18. *The Animals Among Us*, pp. 90–98.
19. See the discussion in Bradshaw, *The Animals Among Us*, pp. 94–7.
20. www.humanesociety.org/resources/animal-cruelty-facts-and-stats; accessed 27 January 2025.
21. Bradshaw, *The Animals Among Us*, p. 67.
22. Michael Joseph, London, 1968.
23. 'The 7 best Tamagotchi and Virtual Pets', 2024, The Spruce Pets, www.thesprucepets.com/best-tamagotchi-virtual-pet-8411788,; accessed 27 January 2025.
24. Andrea Beetz, Kurt Kotrschal, Dennis C. Turner, Karin Hediger, Kerstin Uvnäs-Moberg, and Henri Julius, 'The effect of a real dog, toy dog and friendly person on insecurely attached children during a stressful task: an exploratory study', *Anthrozoös*, 24(4), 2011, pp. 349–68; Andrea Beetz, Henri Julius, Dennis Turner and Kurt Kotrschal, 'Effects of social support by a dog on stress modulation in male children with insecure attachment', *Frontiers in Psychology* 3, 2012, p. 352.

HOME, HEALTH AND LEISURE

1. Bodleian Library, MS Eng. lett. d. 288.
2. American Pet Products Association, *State of the Industry*, 2024.
3. Discussed by Collis Harvey, *The Animal's Companion*, p. 87.
4. Cited in Keith Thomas, *Man and the Natural World: A History of Modern Sensibility*, Pantheon, New York, 1983, p. 105. For discussion, see Collis Harvey, *The Animal's Companion*, p. 24.
5. Cited and discussed in Colliss Harvey, *The Animal's Companion*.
6. All figures are from a variety of links to UK pet statistics at www.statisa.com (accessed 27 January 2025), apart from the UK Pet Food Industry Statistics, at www.ukpetfood.org/information-centre/statistics.html, accessed 31 July 204.
7. Based on estimates from the Office for National Statistics (ONS) Household Finances Survey.

8. 'Growling Tums' pet food advertisement.
9. 'Pamper your fur baby with the world's most expensive luxury pet accessories', Tracy Ann, 19 October 2023, www.prestigeonline.com/hk/style/fashion/most-expensive-luxury-pet-accessories; accessed 27 January 2025. All quotations taken from here.
10. See Gottfried von Strassburg, *Tristan*, trans A. Hatto, Penguin, London, 1974.
11. John Bromyard, *Summa praedicantium*, https://archive.org/details/JohnBromyardSummaPraedicantiumParsPrima1586; accessed 29 June 2025.
12. *Le Livre du Chevalier de la Tour Landry pour l'enseignement de ses filles*, ed. M.A. de Montaiglon, Paris, 1854, pp. 44–6; trans. British Lib MS Harley 1764, printed in *The Book of the Knight of La Tour-Landry*, ed. T. Wright, Kegan Paul, Trench, Trübner & Co., London, 1906, pp. 28–9.
13. General Prologue. 'Wastel breed' is bread made from very-high-quality flour.
14. Jonas Hanway, 'Remarks upon Lapdogs', *A Journal of Eight Days Journey from Portsmouth to Kingston Upon Thames*, 2nd edn, Printed for H. Woodfall, London, 1757, pp. 1.104–5. To similar effect, a modern Islamic website, answering questions about pet ownership, cites as one of the 'Conditions of keeping pets in Islam': 'Not going so far with regard to this matter that it reaches the stage of blameworthy extravagance. We have seen some people who pay thousands and even millions competing to buy a certain animal or take care of it and provide services for it. Some of them even bequeath some of their wealth to them. In some countries, there are festivals and shows for all kinds of animals, on which huge amounts of money are spent. All of this is foolishness and lack of common sense.' https://islamqa.info/en/answers/124154/keeping-pets-in-islam-allowed.
15. 'The devastating effects of child starvation and malnutrition in Africa and the Middle East', Save the Children, 2024. www.savethechildren.org/us/what-we-do/emergency-response/helping-starving-african-children; accessed 27 January 2025.
16. 2023 World Pet Obesity Awareness: Purina Veterinary Nutritionist Dr Jason Gagne: www.petobesityprevention.org/articlesandnews/2023petobesityawareness; accessed 27 January 2025.
17. Albertus Magnus, *On Animals*, trans. Kenneth Kitchell and Irven Resnick, Ohio State University Press, Columbus OH, 2018, p. 1463.
18. Advertisement from Brocklehursts of Bakewell, Derbyshire.
19. 'New study reveals animals can relieve our stress levels', BBC, 22 September 2020. www.bbc.co.uk/newsround/54245971; accessed 27 January 2025.
20. Nikki Harper, 'Pets do reduce stress: new study shows cortisol reduction', 2019, https://wakeup-world.com/2019/08/07/pets-do-reduce-stress-new-study-shows-cortisol-reduction; accessed 27 January 2025.
21. Kerri E. Rodriguez, Crystal I. Bryce, Douglas A. Granger and Marguerite E. O'Haire, 'The effect of a service dog on salivary cortisol awakening response in a military population with posttraumatic stress disorder (PTSD)', *Psychoneuro-endocrinology* 98, 2018, pp. 202–10.
22. Richard Read, 'Alexa, how many dogs come to work at Amazon Seattle? 7000', *LA Times*, 21 June 2019.
23. T. Nagasawa, M. Ohta and H. Uchiyama, 'Effects of the characteristic temperament of cats on the emotions and hemodynamic responses of humans', *PLoS One*, 15(6), 25 June 2020, https://doi.org/10.1371/journal.pone.0235188.
24. James Bowen, *A Street Cat Named Bob: How One Man and His Cat Found Hope on the Streets*, Hodder & Stoughton, London, 2012.
25. Richard Godwin, 'Bob the Busking Cat', *Evening Standard*, 20 March 2012.
26. *Our Home Pets: How to Keep Them Well and Happy*, New York, Harper & Brothers, 1894, cited in Grier, *Pets in America*.
27. Thomas Wright, *The Life of William Cowper*, Haskell House, New York, 1892, p. 56.

28. Laure Desvernays, *Les animaux d'agrement*, 1913, cited in Colliss Harvey, *The Animal's Companion*.
29. *The Animals Among Us*, p. 96.
30. Ibid.
31. Ibid.
32. Acquariumnexus.com; accessed 27 January 2025.
33. 'Finding the right dog', Kennel Club, 2024. www.thekennelclub.org.uk/getting-a-dog/are-you-ready/finding-the-right-dog; accessed 27 January 2025.
34. *Memories*, cited in Simon Garfield, *Dog's Best Friend: A Brief History of an Unbreakable Bond*, Weidenfeld & Nicolson, London, 2021.
35. A 2022 survey asked cat owners about their reasons for owning cats. The greatest proportion (37 per cent) said that the cat was for 'company'; 20 per cent (presumably overlapping with the 37 per cent) gave 'feeling less lonely' as a reason. See 'Main reasons why people get a cat in the United Kingdom (UK) as of 2022', www.statista.com/statistics/796992/reasons-for-cat-ownership-united-kingdom-uk; accessed 27 January 2025.
36. Cited in Garfield, *Dog's Best Friend*.
37. 'And the Lord God said, It is not good that the man should be alone; I will make him an help meet for him. And out of the ground the Lord God formed every beast of the field, and every fowl of the air; and brought them unto Adam to see what he would call them: and whatsoever Adam called every living creature, that was the name thereof. And Adam gave names to all cattle, and to the fowl of the air, and to every beast of the field; *but for Adam there was not found an help meet for him*.' Genesis 2: 18–20 (King James Bible), emphasis added.
38. Catullus 2a, translated by Emma Searle and reproduced with permission. The original reads:

    Passer, deliciae meae puellae,
    quicum ludere, quem in sinu tenere,
    cui primum digitum dare appetenti
    et acris solet incitare morsus,
    cum desiderio meo nitenti
    carum nescio quid lubet iocari,
    et solaciolum sui doloris,
    credo, ut tum gravis acquiescat ardor:
    tecum ludere sicut ipsa possem
    et tristis animi levare curas!
39. Plutarch, *Pericles*, ch. 1, sect. 1.
40. 'Pope Francis says choosing pets over kids is selfish', BBC, 5 January 2022. www.bbc.co.uk/news/world-europe-59884801; accessed 27 January 2025.
41. All citations from Siobhan Smith, 'Meet the people who view their pets as 'substitute children' – and why there's nothing selfish about it', *Metro*, 8 January 2022. https://metro.co.uk/2022/01/08/meet-the-people-who-view-their-pets-as-substitute-children-15881778; accessed 27 January 2025.
42. Sigmund Freud, letter to Marie Bonaparte, 6 December 1936, https://pep-web.org/browse/document/zbk.051.0434a.
43. J.R. Ackerley, *My Father and Myself*, New York Review of Books, New York, 1968, pp. 216–17.
44. At the annual conference of the Association of Pet Behaviour Counsellors, 20 April 2024. Cited in Josh Loeb, 'Are pets replacing children?', *Veterinary Record*, 4(11), May 2024, p. 329. See too Jemma Forman, Louise Brown, Holly Root-Gutteridge, Graham Hole, Raffaela Lesch, Katarzyna Pisanski and David Reby. 'The Puss in Boots effect: dog eye size influences pet-directed speech in women', *Interaction*

Studies, 24(1), 2023, pp. 48–65; James A. Serpell, 'How happy is your pet? The problem of subjectivity in the assessment of companion animal welfare.' *Animal Welfare*, 28(1), 2019, pp. 57–66.

45. Sandy Eckstein, 'Pets in your bed', WebMD, 29 April 2012, www.webmd.com/pets/features/pets-in-your-bed; accessed 27 January 2025.
46. Bradshaw, *The Animals Among Us*, p. 60.
47. 2004 Pet Owner Survey, American Animal Hospital Association, www.aahanet.org/PublicDocuments/petownersurvey2004.pdf; accessed 25 July 2024.
48. See too Sam Wollaston, '"He chose the dog over me": the pets that ruined relationships – from pups interrupting sex to aggressive pigs', *Guardian,* 27 July 2024, www.theguardian.com/lifeandstyle/article/2024/jul/27/he-chose-the-dog-over-me-the-pets-that-ruined-relationships-from-pups-interrupting-sex-to-aggressive-pigs; accessed 27 January 2025.
49. Garfield, *Dog's Best Friend*, p. 18.

THE WORLD OF WORK

1. There seems to be a more or less insatiable appetite for television programmes about dogs and other pets. Take, for example, *Dogs Behaving Badly*, which has aired on UK Channels 4 and 5 since 2017, reaching 10.2 million viewers, and has an Australian iteration, *Dogs Behaving (Very) Badly Australia.* Or *Supervet* (Channel 4: 33 million viewers since 2014), which follows the work of referral vet Noel Pitzpatrick and his team as they deal with complex small-animal veterinary cases.
2. 'Doggy day care', Blue Cross, www.bluecross.org.uk/advice/dog/wellbeing-and-care/doggy-day-care www.bluecross.org.uk/advice/dog/wellbeing-and-care/doggy-day-care; accessed 27 January 2025.
3. Discussed in detail in K. Walker-Meikle, *Mediaeval Pets*, Boydell Press, Woodbridge, 2012, p. 170.
4. 'The Student and His Cat', trans. Robin Flowers, in *The Poem-Book of the Gael*, ed. Eleanor Hull, Browne & Howell, Chicago IL, 1913, pp. 132–3.
5. Oxford, New College MS. ff 88a and 88b, cited and translated in G.C. Coulton, *Social Life in Britain from the Conquest to the Reformation*, Cambridge University Press, Cambridge, 1918, p. 397, discussed in Walker-Meikle, *Mediaeval Pets,* pp. 141–2.
6. Letter from Dan Nicholas Clement, April 1536, in *The Lisle Letters: An Abridgement*, ed. Bridget Boland, from the original edition edited by Muriel St Clare Byrne, University of Chicago Press, Chicago IL, 1983, p. xv; discussed in Colliss Harvey, *The Animal's Companion*, p. 43.
7. The fourteenth-century statutes of New College and All Souls prohibited any kind of dog. In the fifteenth century ferrets were added to the list of proscribed animals: *Statutes of the Colleges of Oxford*, J.H. Parker, Oxford, 1853, vol. 1, ch. 5, p. 48 and ch. 7, p. 44. Discussed in Walker-Meikle, *Mediaeval Pets*, p. 147.
8. Historiches Archiv der Stadt Koln Best, 7004, 249, fol. 68r, discussed in Colliss Harvey, *The Animal's Companion*, p. 198.
9. Cited in Garfield, *Dog's Best Friend*, p. 146.
10. Cited in ibid., p. 153.
11. www.statista.com/statistics/304028/leading-toilet-paper-brands-in-the-uk.
12. G.J. Golan and L. Zaidner, 'Creative strategies in viral advertising: an application of Taylor's six-segment message strategy wheel', *Journal of Computer-Mediated Communication*, 13(4), 2008, pp. 959–72.
13. C. Tomkovick, R. Yelkur and L. Christians, 'The USA's biggest marketing event

keeps getting bigger: an in-depth look at Super Bowl advertising in the 1990s', *Journal of Marketing Communications*, 7(2), 2001, pp. 89–108.

14. N. Spears and R. Germain, '1900–2000 in review: the shifting role and face of animals in print advertisements in the twentieth century', *Journal of Advertising*, 36(3), 2007, pp. 19–33; S. Brown, 'Where the wild brands are: some thoughts on anthropomorphic marketing', *The Marketing Review*, 10(3), 2010, pp. 209–24.
15. Barbara Keller and Heribert Gierl, 'Effectiveness of animal images in advertising', *Marketing ZFP*, 42(1), 2020, pp. 3–32.
16. 'Buying pets on a whim, with no research, could be causing mental and physical misery for millions of companion animals, warns PDSA', 26 September 2018, www.pdsa.org.uk/press-office/latest-news/buying-pets-on-a-whim-with-no-research-could-be-causing-mental-and-physical-misery-for-millions-of-companion-animals-warns-pdsa; accessed 27 January 2025.
17. Jennifer Hagen, Renate Weller, Timothy Mair, and Tierney Kinnison, 'Investigation of factors affecting recruitment and retention in the UK veterinary profession', *Veterinary Record* 187, 2020.

SOCIETY, POLITICS AND WAR

1. 'Native American totem animals and their meanings', n.d., www.legendsofamerica.com/na-totems; accessed 27 January 2025.
2. 'Your totem animal encounters', n.d., https://helektrahealing.com/en/spd/009/Your-Totem-Animal-Encounters; accessed 27 January 2025.
3. Hobgood-Oster, *A Dog's History of the World*, p. 32.
4. Cited in Plutarch's *Life of Marius*.
5. Emmanuel Levinas, 'The Name of a Dog, or Natural Rights', in *Difficult Freedom: Essays in Judaism*, trans. Seán Hand, Johns Hopkins University Press, Baltimore MD, 1990, p. 153; cited in Hobgood-Oster, *A Dog's History of the World*, p. 103.
6. Michael Morpurgo, *War Horse*, Kaye & Ward, London, 1982.
7. As did the geese whose honking saved Rome from the Gauls in the fourth century BCE. The grateful Romans erected a temple to Juno, in which geese were regarded as sacred birds.
8. After the Vietnam War many handlers of US military dogs tried to adopt them rather than seeing them abandoned or destroyed. Only in 2000 was a law passed permitting the adoption of military dogs.
9. Graham Greene records such an incident in Berkhamsted: see his autobiography, *A Sort of Life*, Bodley Head, London, 1971.
10. Garfield, *Dog's Best Friend*, p. 50.
11. www.bma.org.uk/news-and-opinion/the-queen-the-surgeon-and-a-box-of-dog-biscuits; accessed 27 January 2025.
12. See Nathan J. Robinson, 'Puppaganda: how politicians use pets to convince you of their humanity', *Current Affairs*, 15 January 2021, www.currentaffairs.org/news/2021/01/dogaganda-how-politicians-use-pets-to-convince-you-of-their-humanity; accessed 27 January 2025.
13. Ibid.
14. Hitler was a lifelong dog lover, who nonetheless used his final dog, Blondi, to test one of his suicide capsules. It worked.
15. Pliny the Elder, *Natural History*, 9.39; Seneca the Younger, *On Clemency*, 1.18.2. The 'lampreys' may actually have been moray eels, but that hardly revives his reputation.
16. *De Pallio*, trans Vincent Hunlink, Brill, Leiden, 2005.
17. Cited in Colliss Harvey, *The Animal's Companion*, p. 197.

RELIGION AND RITES OF PASSAGE

1. David Lewis-Williams, *The Mind in the Cave: Consciousness and the Origins of Art*, Thames & Hudson, London, 2002.
2. Exodus 22: 18, King James Version.
3. See Walker-Meikle, *Mediaeval Pets*, p. 30.
4. Translation at https://franciscanfriarscresson.org/the-canticle-of-the-sun; accessed 27 January 2025.
5. Another example of Jesus using animals to make a point is recorded in the late second-century Infancy Gospel of Thomas, the Quran, the mediaeval Jewish *Sefer Toledot Yeshu*, and elsewhere, where Jesus makes clay birds which he then brings to life: see the Infancy Gospel of Thomas 2:1–3 and Quran 3.49 and 5.10. There are various iterations of the *Sefer Toledot Yeshu*, making exact citation impossible. There are other references to the story in, for example, the Arabic Infancy Gospel and the Latin Gospel of Pseudo-Matthew. For discussion, see Sarit Kattan Gribetz, 'Jesus and the clay birds: Reading *Toledot Yeshu* in light of the Infancy Gospels', in *Envisioning Judaism: Studies in Honor of Peter Schäfer*, ed. R. Boustan, K. Hermann, R. Leicht, A. Reed and G. Veltri, with A. Ramos, Mohr Siebeck, Tübingen, 2013, pp. 1021–48.
6. Christopher Smart, *Jubilate Agno*, first published as *Rejoice in the Lamb: A Song from Bedlam*, ed. W.F. Stead, Jonathan Cape, London, 1939.
7. The prayer for silkworms, for instance, includes: 'All-good King, show us even now your loving kindness; and as you blessed the well of Jacob (John 4:6), and the pool of Siloam (John 9:7), and the cup of your holy apostles (Matt. 26:27), so bless also these silkworms; and as you multiplied the stars in heaven and the sand beside the sea-shore, so multiply these silkworms, granting them health and strength: and may they feed without coming to any harm … so that they may produce shrouds of pure silk, to your glory and praise', *Evchologion to Mega*, ed. N.P. Papadopoulos, Saliveros, Athens, n.d., p. 511.
8. Jennifer Young, 'All creatures great and small', *Untapped New York*, 2016, https://untappedcities.com/2016/10/03/all-creatures-great-and-small-blessing-the-animals-at-new-yorks-largest-cathedral; accessed 27 January 2025; Scott Lynch, 'Inside NYC's very cute animal blessing at St John the Divine', *Gothamist*, 2 October 2017, https://gothamist.com/arts-entertainment/inside-nycs-very-cute-animal-blessing-at-st-john-the-divine#photo-1; accessed 27 January 2025.
9. www.nationalchurchestrust.org/explore/promote/paws-pews.
10. See Christopher Howse, 'Sacred mysteries: What's wrong with taking your dog to church', *Daily Telegraph*, 9 March 2024.
11. 'Paws in pews', National Churches Trust, n.d., www.nationalchurchestrust.org/explore/promote/paws-pews; accessed 27 January 2025.
12. Crows and ravens are similarly celebrated on day one of the festival, and cattle on days three and four. Prayers are also addressed to cows during *Gopastami* – part of Diwali.
13. See www.ayurvedajournals.com/article/karni-mata-rat-temple.
14. See Exodus 12:38 for the reference to the Israelites' animals.
15. 'How to throw a bark mitzvah for your dog', *Dogtime*, 22 August 2023, https://dogtime.com/lifestyle/parties/507–bark-mitzvah-dog-parties; accessed 27 January 2025.
16. The list of suggested hymns is 'All Creatures of Our God and King', 'All Things Bright and Beautiful', 'For the Beauty of the Earth', 'Morning Has Broken', 'If I Were a Butterfly, 'Think of a World Without Any Flowers', 'The Lord of Sea and Sky', 'Let There Be Love Shared Among Us', 'Make Me a Channel of Your Peace' and 'On Eagles' Wings'.

17. All citations from 'An Order for a Pets' Service', www.nationalpetmonth.org.uk/downloads/pet%20service.pdf; accessed 27 January 2025.
18. 'St Francis Day Survival Guide: Practical Tips for Animal Blessings', *Building Faith*, n.d., www.buildfaith.org/st-francis-day-survival-guide-blessing-the-animals/#gref.
19. 'Tips for holding a "blessing of the animals" service', Five Leaf Eco-Awards, n.d., https://fiveleafecoawards.org/resources/tips-for-holding-a-blessing-of-the-animals-service; accessed 27 January 2025.
20. Gail Gilmore, *Dog Church*, Primal Nutrition, Dallas TX, 2017.
21. And the multi-headed dog, Cerberus, prevented the dead from leaving Hades once they had got there.
22. Julia Castenada, *Dog Church*, Dog Day Afternoon, Topeka KS, 2018.
23. Amazon.com reviews: www.amazon.com/Dog-Church-Julie-Castaneda/product-reviews/0692140727/ref=cm_cr_dp_d_show_all_btm?ie=UTF8&reviewerType=all_reviews; accessed 27 January 2025.
24. Homily 82, in *Mystic Treatises by Isaac of Nineveh*, trans. A.J. Wensinck, Koninklijke Akademie van Wetenschappen, Amsterdam, 1923, p. 386; translation adapted by Bishop Kallistos Ware in 'Compassion for Animals in the Orthodox Church, 2019, http://panorthodoxconcernforanimals.org/uncategorized/compassion-for-animals-in-the-orthodox-church/#_ftn5; accessed 27 January 2025.

THEIR ENDS AND OURS

1. Diary, 18 December 1825.
2. Diary, 8 April 1663.
3. Catullus 3, translated by Emma Searle and reproduced with permission. The original reads:

   Lugete, o Veneres Cupidinesque,
   et quantumst hominum venustiorum
   passer mortuus est meae puellae,
   passer, deliciae meae puellae,
   quem plus illa oculis suis amabat:
   nam mellitus erat suamque norat
   ipsam tam bene quam puella matrem;
   nec sese a gremio illius movebat,
   sed circumsiliens modo huc modo illuc
   ad solam dominam usque pipiabat
   qui nunc it per iter tenebricosum illuc,
   unde negant redire quemquam
   at vobis male sit, malae tenebrae
   Orci, quae omnia bella devoratis:
   tam bellum mihi passerem abstulistis
   o factum male! o miselle passer!
   tua nunc opera meae puellae
   flendo turgiduli rubent ocelli.
4. Garfield, *Dog's Best Friend*, p. 6.
5. Alexis Fleming, 'Experience: I run a hospice for animals', *Guardian*, 7 September 2018, www.theguardian.com/lifeandstyle/2018/sep/07/experience-i-run-a-hospice-for-animals; accessed 27 January 2025.
6. 'Meet our Vets2Home Team', www.peacefulpetgoodbyes.uk/our-team; accessed 27 January 2025
7. Evelyn Waugh, *The Loved One: An Anglo-American Tragedy*, Chapman & Hall, London, 1948, chapters 2 and 7.

8. For further discussion of the symbolic use to which 'Michael Field' put Whym Chow, see Caroline Baylis-Green, 'Sentimental coatings and the subversive pet closet: Michael Field's Whym Chow: Flame of Love', 2018, www.torch.ox.ac.uk/article/sentimental-coatings-and-the-subversive-pet-closet-michael-fields-whym-chow-flame-of-love; accessed 27 January 2025.
9. https://editions.covecollective.org/edition/whym-chow-flame-love/whym-chow-flame-love.
10. Lizzie Edmonds, 'Kate Beckinsale reveals second tattoo in tribute to late cat, Clive', *Evening Standard*, 1 September 2023.
11. Gemma Peplow, 'Pet loss and grief', *Sky News*, 7 October 2023. https://news.sky.com/story/pet-loss-and-grief-my-world-crashed-the-rising-number-of-people-seeking-support-over-the-deaths-of-their-animals-12974903; accessed 27 January 2025.
12. George Reisner, 'The dog which was honored by the King of Upper and Lower Egypt', *Bulletin of the Museum of Fine Arts*, 34(206), December 1936, pp. 96–9.
13. Ercole Strozzi, 'Carmina borgetti canis', in *Carmina illustrum poetarum Italorum,* vol. 3, pp. 181–7; discussed in Walker-Meikle, *Mediaeval Pets*, p. 147.
14. 'Canzone nella Perdita d'una gatta', in Francesco Coppetta Beccuti and Giovanni Guidiccioni, *Rime*, ed E. Chiorboli, Bari, 1912, pp. 307–10; see Walker-Meikle, *Mediaeval Pets*, p. 196.
15. Photograph in Daniel Meadows archive, Bodleian. MS. Meadows 177.
16. *The Boke of Phyllyp Sparowe*, [R. Copland] for [R. Kele], London [1545?]. *STC* 22594. Skelton's dates are 1460–1529. The date of composition of the *Boke* is unknown.
17. 'Did you know pets can visit the hospice?' Dovehouse Hospice, n.d., www.dovehouse.org.uk/about-us/news/did-you-know-pets-can-visit-the-hospice; accessed 27 January 2025.
18. Neal Hopkin, 'Should you bring pets to visit in hospice care?', Suncrest Care, 25 May 2021, www.suncrestcare.com/should-you-bring-pets-to-visit-in-hospice-care; accessed 27 January 2025.
19. *Greyfriars Bobby: The Most Faithful Dog in the World*, Amberley Publishing, Stroud, 2011.
20. Peter Seddon, 'Faithful Tip's 105-day vigil next to his fallen master touched the hearts of a nation', *Derbyshire Telegraph*, 21 February 2018, www.derbytelegraph.co.uk/news/nostalgia/faithful-tips-105–day-vigil-1242193; accessed 27 January 2025.
21. *Iliad*, book 23.
22. The surviving corgis were in fact adopted by members of the royal family. King Edward VII's terrier, Caesare, followed, but did not enter, his master's coffin.
23. Epistles 4.2.3.
24. 'Staindrop Church – a Neville Mausoleum', in *A Mediaeval Potpourri*, 2022, https://sparkypus.com/2022/06/02/staindrop-church-mausoleum-of-the-nevilles; accessed 27 January 2025.
25. For a detailed review of dog burials in antiquity, see Hobgood-Oster, *A Dog's History of the World*, ch. 2, and Bradshaw, *The Animals Among Us*, ch. 1.
26. Other ancient pet cemeteries are more mysterious. Over one thousand dogs were interred in the dedicated fifth-century BCE dog cemetery in Ashkelon. They do not seem to have been sacrificed; some had died of natural causes. Other fifth-century Phoenician dog cemeteries are known. They are much, and inconclusively, discussed.
27. Doing something like the same job, stone dogs, no doubt intended to look like the faithful dogs of the manor, lie at the feet of the effigies of many a European knight and his lady.

    Even if the deceased's own pet could not join them in the underworld, there are examples in many mythologies of *some* animals being present. The multi-headed dog

Cerberus prevented escape from Hades, and in the *Rig Veda* the king of the dead, Yama, has two dogs at his side. The dead run past them to join the ancestors.

28. 'Compassion for animals in the Orthodox Church', *International Journal of Orthodox Theology*, 10(2), 2019, www.orthodox-theology.com/media/PDF/2.2019/MetropolitanKallistosWare.pdf; accessed 27 January 2025.
29. 'Do animals go to heaven? The Bible's answer', *Watchtower*, n.d., https://wol.jw.org/en/wol/d/r1/lp-e/502019179; accessed 27 January 2025.
30. See Isaiah 11:6–9. This is more or less the view of John Wesley: 'But will "the creature", will even the brute creation, always remain in this deplorable condition [of frustration, as described in Romans 8: 19–21]? God forbid that we should affirm this; yea, or even entertain such a thought! While "the whole creation groaneth together", (whether men attend or not,) their groans are not dispersed in idle air, but enter into the ears of Him that made them. … He seeth "the earnest expectation" wherewith the whole animated creation "waiteth for" that final "manifestation of the sons of God;" in which "they themselves also shall be delivered" (not by annihilation; annihilation is not deliverance) "from the" present 'bondage of corruption, into" a measure of "the glorious liberty of the children of God." … Nothing can be more express: Away with vulgar prejudices, and let the plain word of God take place. They "shall be delivered from the bondage of corruption, into glorious liberty", even a measure, according as they are capable, of "the liberty of the children of God".' John Calvin agreed: 'Thus the condemnation of mankind is imprinted on the heavens, and on the earth, and on all creatures. It hence also appears to what excelling glory the sons of God shall be exalted; for all creatures shall be renewed in order to amplify it, and to render it illustrious'; as did Billy Graham, who, when asked if a questioner would meet their pet in heaven, said: 'I do not believe that Scripture gives us any direct answer about this, although many Bible scholars believe there will be animals in heaven.… There is one thing you can be certain of, however: [God] wants us to be completely happy in Heaven – and we will be. Therefore if God knows we will be happier because there will be animals with us in Heaven, then you can be assured He will do what is best for us.'
31. *The Problem of Pain*, Centenary Press, London, 1940.
32. Pope Francis' second encyclical, 2015.
33. *The Last Will and Testament of an Extremely Distinguished Dog*, 17 December 1940. https://web.archive.org/web/20140223130954; www.eoneill.com/texts/blemie/contents.htm; accessed 27 January 2025.
34. By Greg Harper – apparently Woolly's owner.
35. The tone of these memorials is very similar to that in the book of poems of 'Michael Field', all directed to their dead Chow, which we saw earlier. One poem, 'Introit', says:

    O Chow, my little Love, thou art come home.
    No creature in more state.
    Dead to the haunts of life hath even come.
    And, little Love, the great.
    Almighty Power, almightier than the dome.
    Beyond all stars, or than Time's hoariest date.
    Or sea or the world's rock hath brought thee home.
36. Eric Tourigny, 'Do all dogs go to Heaven? Tracking human–animal relationships through the archaeological survey of pet cemeteries', *Antiquity*, 94(378), 2020, pp. 1614–29.
37. There is a large collection in Elliott O'Donnell, *Animal Ghosts, or Animal Hauntings and the Hereafter*, William Rider & Son, London, 1913. It includes cats, dogs, horses,

cattle, goats, sheep, pigs, apes, rabbits, elephants, lions, tigers and birds. See too Ed Anderson, 'Animal ghosts', *Evidence of Animal Afterlife*, 26 November 2020, https://evidenceofanimalafterlife.com/animal-ghosts, accessed 27 January 2025; and Romany Reagan, 'Spectral animals: ghost pets to hellhounds', Blackthorn & Stone, 16 April 2020, https://blackthornandstone.com/2020/04/16/spectral-animals-ghost-pets-to-hellhounds, accessed 27 January 2025.

38. Cited O'Donnell, *Animal Ghosts.*
39. Kim Sheridan, *Animals and the Afterlife.*
40. Psychic, 'Essential facts about animal ghost encounters', n.d., www.keen.com/articles/psychic/fluffy-is-that-you-essential-facts-about-animal-ghost-encounters; accessed 27 January 2025.
41. ViaGen Pets and Equine, n.d. www.viagenpets.com; accessed 27 January 2025.
42. ViaGen Pets and Equine, Ceaser: www.viagenpets.com/story/ceaser; accessed 27 January 2025.
43. Viagen Pets and Equine, Rumbler: www.viagenpets.com/story/rumbler; accessed 27 January 2025.
44. For discussion of the ethics, see Jacob Brogan, 'The real reasons you shouldn't clone your dog', *Smithsonian Magazine*, 22 March 2018, www.smithsonianmag.com/science-nature/why-cloning-your-dog-so-wrong; accessed 27 January 2025.
45. All citations from Cuddleclones: https://cuddleclones.com; accessed 27 January 2025. There are other companies in the market: see, for instance, Petsies: www.mypetsies.com; accessed 27 January 2025.

PEOPLE AND THEIR PETS

1. Hobgood-Oster, *A Dog's History of the World*, p. 49.
2. See Garfield, *Dog's Best Friend*, p. 9.
3. Colliss Harvey, *The Animal's Companion*, p. 135.
4. www.butternutbox.com.
5. *Childe Harold's Pilgrimage.*
6. For further discussion, see Collis Harvey, *The Animal's Companion*, p. 21.
7. Steingo, *Interspecies Communication*, p. 87.
8. There are always exceptions. The Polynesians of Samoa, for instance, kept tame eels in holes in the ground, and trained them to come to the surface when they heard a whistle. See Bradshaw, *The Animals Among Us*, p. 26.
9. *Ring of Bright Water*, Longman, London, 1960; *The Rocks Remain,* Longman, London, 1963; *Raven Seek Thy Brother,* Longman, London, 1968.
10. There may be another, more dubious use, operating deeper down in our psyches. We know that we shouldn't really be tame – we're ashamed of it – and we *blame* our pets for taming us. We keep dogs, cats, pythons and canaries as reminders of what we really are, as ways of insisting that we're like that still, and, when that fails, as scape-dogs, scape-cats, scape-snakes and scape-birds, at fault for stopping us being more the way we should be.

Further reading

As implied in the Preface, there's a good case for saying that everything ever written about humans and non-humans should be on a list of further reading, and a good case for saying that nothing ever written by humans about anything should be on the list – because any list that falls short of an infinite catalogue of facts and an infallible compendium of wise reflection is bound to misrepresent dangerously.

I doubt, therefore, that there is a good case for the list below, but here it is anyway.

I have been particularly helped by John Bradshaw's *The Animals Among Us: The New Science of Anthrozoology*; Keggie Carew's *Beastly: A New History of Animals and Us*; Jacky Colliss Harvey's *The Animal's Companion: People and Their Pets, a 26,000-Year Love Story*; Stanley Coren's *The Pawprints of History: Dogs and the Course of Human Events*; Simon Garfield's *Dog's Best Friend: A Brief History of an Unbreakable Bond*; Katherine Grier's *Pets in America: A History*; Jay Griffiths's *How Animals Heal Us*; Laura Hobgood-Oster's *A Dog's History of the World: Canines and the Domestication of Humans*; Jules Howard's *Wonderdog: How the Science of Dogs Changed the Science of Life*; and Kathleen Walker-Meikle's *Mediaeval Pets.*

Bailey, Paul, *A Dog's Life*, Hamish Hamilton, London, 2003.
Bekoff, Marc, *The Emotional Lives of Animals,* New World Library, Novato CA, 2007.
Berns, Gregory, *How Dogs Love Us*, Houghton Mifflin Harcourt, Boston MA and New York, 2013.
Bondeson, Jan, *Amazing Dogs: A Cabinet of Canine Curiosities*, Amberley, 2011.
Bowron, E.P., Carolyn Rose Rebbert, Robert Rosenblum and William Secord, *Best in Show: The Dog in Art from the Renaissance to Today*, Yale University Press, New Haven CT, 2006.
Bradshaw, John, *In Defence of Dogs*, Penguin, London, 2012.

Bradshaw, John, *The Animals Among Us: The New Science of Anthrozoology*, Allen Lane, London, 2017.
Budinsky, Stephen, *The Truth About Dogs*, Weidenfeld & Nicolson, London, 2001.
Caius, John, *Of Englishe Dogges, the Diversities, the Names, the Natures, and the Properties: A Short Treatise Written in Latine*, Vintage Dog Books, London, 2005.
Carew, Keggie, *Beastly: A New History of Animals and Us*, Canongate, Edinburgh, 2023.
Carr, Neil, *Domestic Animals and Leisure*, Palgrave Macmillan, London, 2015.
Clutton-Brock, Juliet, *A Natural History of Domesticated Mammals*, Cambridge University Press, Cambridge, 1999.
Colliss Harvey, J., *The Animal's Companion: People and Their Pets, a 26,000-Year Love Story*, Allen & Unwin, London, 2019.
Coppinger, Raymond, and Mark Feinstein, *How Dogs Work*, University of Chicago Press, Chicago IL, 2015.
Coren, Stanley, *How to Speak Dog: Mastering the Art of Dog–Human Communication*, Simon & Schuster, New York, 2001.
Coren, Stanley, *The Pawprints of History: Dogs and the Course of Human Events*, Free Press, New York, 2002.
DeMello, Margo, *Animals and Society: An Introduction To Human–Animal Studies*, Columbia University Press, New York, 2012.
DeMello, Margo, *Mourning Animals: Rituals and Practices Surrounding Animal Death*, Michigan University Press, Ann Arbor MI, 2016.
Derr, Mark, *Dog's Best Friend*, University of Chicago Press, Chicago IL, 2004.
Fagan, Brian, *The Intimate Bond: How Animals Shaped Human History*, Bloomsbury, London and New York, 2015.
Francis, Richard C., *Domesticated: Evolution in a Man-made World*, W.W. Norton, New York, 2015.
Franklin, Jon, *The Wolf in the Parlor: The Eternal Connection between Humans and Dogs*, Henry Holt, New York, 2009.
Garfield, S., *Dog's Best Friend: A Brief History of an Unbreakable Bond*, Weidenfeld & Nicolson, London, 2021.
Grandin, Temple, and Catherine Johnson, *Animals Make Us Human*, Houghton Mifflin Harcourt, Boston MA and New York, 2009.
Gray, Beryl, *The Dog in the Dickensian Imagination*, Ashgate, Farnham, 2014.
Green, Susie, *Dogs in Art*, Reaktion Books, London, 2019.
Grenier, Roger, *The Difficulty of Being a Dog*, University of Chicago Press, Chicago IL, 2000.
Grier, K.C., *Pets in America: A History*, University of North Carolina Press, Chapel Hill NC, 2006.
Griffiths, Jay, *How Animals Heal Us*, Hamish Hamilton, London, 2025.
Hamlett, Jane, and Julie-Marie Strange, *Pet Revolution: Animals and the Making of Modern British Life*, Reaktion, London, 2023.
Haraway, Donna, *The Companion Species Manifesto: Dogs, People and Significant Otherness*, Prickly Paradigm Press, Chicago IL, 2003.
Haraway, Donna, *When Species Meet*, University of Minnesota Press, Minneapolis MI, 2008.
Hausman, Gerald and Loretta, *The Mythology of Dogs*, St Martin's Press, New York, 1997.
Hawtree, Christopher, *The Literary Companion to Dogs*, Sinclair-Stevenson, London 1993.
Herzog, Hal, *Some We Love, Some We Hate, Some We Eat: Why It's So Hard to Think Straight about Animals*, HarperCollins, New York, 2011.
Hobgood-Oster, Laura, *Holy Dogs and Asses: Animals in the Christian Tradition*, University of Illinois Press, Urbana IL, 2008.

Hobgood-Oster, Laura, *The Friends We Keep: Unleashing Christianity's Compassion for Animals*, Baylor University Press, Waco TX, 2010.
Hobgood-Oster, Laura, *A Dog's History of the World: Canines and the Domestication of Humans,* Baylor University Press, Waco TX, 2014.
Homans, John, *What's a Dog For? The Surprising History, Science, Philosophy and Politics of Man's Best Friend*, Penguin, London, 2012.
Horowitz, Alexandra, *Inside of a Dog: What Dogs See, Smell and Know*, Scribner, New York, 2012.
Horowitz, Alexandra, *Our Dogs, Ourselves*, Simon & Schuster, London, 2019.
Howard, J., *Wonderdog: How the Science of Dogs Changed the Science of Life*, Bloomsbury Sigma, London, 2022.
Hurn, Samantha, *Humans and Other Animals: Cross-cultural Perspectives on Human–Animal Interactions*, Pluto Press, London, 2012.
Jackson, Frank, *Faithful Friends: Dogs in Life and Literature*, Robinson, London, 1997.
Jacobs, Millie, *The Pet Loss Guide*, Orion, London, 2022.
Kaloff, Linda, *Looking at Animals in Human History*, Reaktion, London, 2007.
Katz, Jon, *The New Work of Dogs: Tending to Life, Love and Family*, Random House, New York, 2004.
Lemish, Michael G., *War Dogs: A History of Loyalty and Heroism*, Potomac Books, Dulles VA, 1999.
Long, David, *Animal Heroes: Inspiring True Stories of Courageous Animals*, Random House, New York, 2013.
Lorenz, Konrad, *Man Meets Dog*, Methuen, London, 1954.
Losos, Jonathan B., *The Age of Cats: From the Savannah to Your Sofa, the Secret Life and Evolutionary History of the Cat*, William Collins, London, 2023.
Marra, Peter P., and Chris Santella, *Cat Wars: The Devastating Consequences of a Cuddly Killer*, Princeton University Press, Princeton NJ, 2016.
Menzies, Lucy, *The First Friend: An Anthology of the Friendship of Man and Dog Compiled from the Literature of All Ages 1400 B.C.–1921 A.D.*, Allen & Unwin, London, 1922.
Merwin, Henry Childs, *Dogs and Men*, Houghton Mifflin, Boston MA and New York, 1910.
Miklósi, Ádám, *Dog: Behaviour, Evolution and Cognition*, Oxford University Press, Oxford, 2007.
Miklósi, Ádám, *The Dog: A Natural History*, Ivy Press, Brighton, 2018.
Morey, Darcy, *Dogs: Domestication and Development of a Social Bond*, Cambridge University Press, Cambridge, 2010.
Murray, Dawn, *An Introduction to Pet Bereavement Counselling*, independently published, 2023.
Newcombe, Emily, *Losing a Pet: A Book of Grief and Recovery*, independently published, 2024.
Pierce, Jessica, *The Last Walk: Reflections on Our Pets at the End of Their Lives*, University of Chicago Press, Chicago IL, 2012.
Ritvo, Harriet, *The Animal Estate: The English and Other Creatures in the Victorian Age*, Harvard University Press, Cambridge MA, 1987.
Rogers, Katharine M., *First Friend: A History of Dogs and Humans*, St Martin's Press, New York, 2005.
Rosenblum, Robert, *The Dog in Art from Rococo to Post-modernism*, Abrams, New York, 1988.
Schaffer, Michael, *One Nation Under Dog*, Henry Holt, New York, 2009.
Schwartz, Marion, *A History of Dogs in the Early Americas*, Yale University Press, New Haven CT, 1998.

Serpell, James, *The Domestic Dog: Its Evolution, Behaviour and Interactions with People*, Cambridge University Press, Cambridge, 1995.
Serpell, James, *In the Company of Animals: A Study of Human–Animal Relationships*, Cambridge University Press, Cambridge, 1996.
Sheldrake, Rupert, *Dogs that Know When Their Owners Are Coming Home*, Hutchinson, London, 1999.
Shipman, Pat, *Our Oldest Companions: The Story of the First Dogs*, Harvard University Press, Cambridge MA, 2021.
Smith, Kate, *Guides, Guards and Gifts to the Gods: Domesticated Dogs in the Art and Archaeology of Iron Age and Roman Britain*, Archaeopress, Oxford, 2006.
Sorenson, John, and Atsuko Matsuoka, eds, *Dog's Best Friend? Rethinking Canid–Human Relations*, McGill–Queen's University Press, Montreal QC and Kingston ON, 2019.
Steingo, Gavin, *Interspecies Communication: Sound and Music beyond Humanity*, University of Chicago Press, Chicago IL, 2024.
Tague, Ingrid H., *Animal Companions: Pets and Social Change in Eighteenth-Century Britain*, Penn State University Press, University Park PA, 2015.
Tesdell, Diana Secker (ed.), *Dog Stories*, Everyman, London, 2010.
Tesdell, Diana Secker (ed.), *Cat Stories*, Everyman, London, 2011.
Thomas, Elizabeth Marshall, *The Hidden Life of Dogs*, Houghton Mifflin, New York, 1993.
Thurston, Elizabeth M., *The Lost History of the Canine Race*, Andrews & McMeel, Kansas City KS, 1996.
Vesey-Fitzgerald, Brian, *The Domestic Dog: An Introduction to Its History*, Routledge, London, 1957.
Walker-Meikle, Kathleen, *Mediaeval Pets*, Boydell Press, Woodbridge, 2012.
Wang, Xiaoming, and Richard H.Tedford, *Dogs: Their Fossil Relatives and Evolutionary History*, Columbia University Press, New York, 2008.
Webb, Stephen, *On God and Dogs: A Christian Theology of Compassion for Animals*, Oxford University Press, Oxford, 1998.
White, David, *Myths of the Dog-Man*, University of Chicago Press, Chicago IL, 1991.
Worboys, Michael, Julie-Marie Strange and Neil Pemberton, *The Invention of the Modern Dog: Breed and Blood in Victorian Britain*, Johns Hopkins University Press, Baltimore MD, 2018.

PICTURE CREDITS

1 Metropolitan Museum of Art, New York, Gift of Helen Miller Gould, 1910 10.130.1332
2 The J. Paul Getty Museum, Villa Collection, Malibu, California, 71.AA.271
3 Wikimedia Commons: https://commons.wikimedia.org/wiki/File:Cave_canem_MAN_Napoli_Inv110666.jpg
4 Bodleian Library, MS. Ashmole 1511, fol. 25v
5 Bodleian Library, MS. Ashmole 1511, fol. 9r
6 Bodleian Library, MS. Douce 264, fol. 21r
7 Bridgeman/Museo Civico, Turin
8 Bodleian Library, MS. Bodl. 764, fol. 51r
9 https://commons.wikimedia.org/wiki/File:Monte_Oliveto_Madjore.jpg, photo by VIRan, CC BY-SA 4.0
10 Metropolitan Museum of Art, New York, Fletcher Fund, 1919, 19.73.1
11 Ashmolean Museum, University of Oxford, WA1846.239
12 Metropolitan Museum of Art, New York, The Cloisters Collection, 1999, 1999.243
13 Ashmolean Museum, University of Oxford, WA1956.15
14 Bodleian Library, MS. Ashmole 1504, fol. 34v
15 Bodleian Library, MS. Bodl. Or. 430, fol. 177r
16 Bodleian Library, MS. Don. e. 192, fol. 55
17 Metropolitan Museum of Art. New York, Gift of Mr. and Mrs. Charles Wrightsman, 1971 1971.206.18
18 Bodleian Library, MS. Ouseley Add. 166, fol. 13
19 Bodleian Library, MS. Ouseley 297, fol. 4r
20 Ashmolean Museum, University of Oxford, EA2007.146
21 Bodleian Library, John Johnson Collection: Music Titles 8
22 Bodleian Library, John Johnson Collection: Window Bills and Advertisements folder 3 (36)
23 Bodleian Library, John Johnson Collection: Prospectuses16 (46)
24 Bodleian Library, John Johnson Collection: Scraps 4 (3)
25 J.T. Vintage/Bridgeman Images GLH1200933
26 Bodleian Library, John Johnson Collection: Soap 1 (26b)
27 Bodleian Library, Rec. d. 602, cover
28 Bodleian Library, MS. Eng. misc. c. 304
29 Bodleian Library, MS. Minn 176
30 © Imperial War Museum (Q 12039), 12039
31 Bodleian Library, MS. 19966/68
32 Carol M. Highsmith Archive, Library of Congress, Prints and Photographs Division.
33 Bodleian Library, N. 2706 d.10 vol 138–9 p. 90
34 Bodleian Library, Johnson Adds 421 (Tram Tickets Box 1)
35 Bodleian Library, uncatalogued JJC pets related items
36 Bodleian Library, MS. 19966/97
37 © Stephen Jaffe/Alamy
38 © Daniel Meadows. Bodleian Library, MS. Meadows 177, folder 3
39 © Daniel Meadows. Bodleian Library, MS. Meadows 177, folder 1
40 Courtesy of Exeter College, photo William Lane

Index